The tle Shop of Horrors Book

The Little Shop of Horrors Book

The Complete, Behind-the-scenes Story of the Original Cult Movie, the Off-Broadway Musical and the Second, Blockbuster Film.

John McCarty
Mark Thomas McGee

ST MARTIN'S PRESS
New York

Cover photo credits:
Front: *Top left*   Peter Cunningham;
         Top right Copyright © 1960 The Filmgroup, Inc.;
         Bottom   Copyright © The Geffen Film Company;
Back: Fangoria magazine.

Cover and book design by *In the Can*

Library of Congress Cataloging-in-Publication Data

McCarty, John, 1944-
       The little shop of horrors book / by John McCarty and Mark Thomas
McGee.
       p.   cm.
       ISBN 0-312-01784-7 (pbk.) : $12.95
       1. Little shop of horrors (Motion picture) 2. Little shop of
horrors (Motion picture : 1986) 3. Menken, Alan. Little shop of
horrors.   I. McGee, Mark Thomas, 1947-   . II. Title.
PN1997.L5943M3 1988
791.43'72--dc19   87-38273
                                                       CIP

First Edition
10 9 8 7 6 5 4 3 2 1

For the 908 Beacon Street boys,
who were there when ...
— *JMc*

***

For Wendy Wright and Bob Villard
— *MTM*

Acknowledgments

TELLING THE *COMPLETE* STORY OF *The Little Shop of Horrors* – in *all* its forms – could not have been accomplished without the help, generosity and great patience of the following individuals and organizations. We thank them profusely:

Dominick Abel; Sally Burke; Eric Caidin (Hollywood Book & Poster Company); Roger Corman; Judi Davidson Publicity; The Geffen Film Company; Charles Griffith; Jonathan Haze; Jackie Joseph; Irv Letofsky (*Los Angeles Times*); John P. Lowe; Christopher McCarty; Dave McDonnell; Dick Miller; Stuart Moore (St. Martin's Press); Karen Richardson (St. Martin's Press); R.J. Robertson; John P. Ryan; Solters, Roskin/Friedman, Inc. Public Relations; Jim Stewart; Anthony Timpone; Robert Tolan; Warner Bros. Pictures.

Contents

Foreword by
Roger Corman

The LITTLE SHOP OF HORRORS

THE FUNNIEST PICTURE THIS YEAR!

A rare lobby card from the original The Little Shop of Horrors.

I BELIEVE I HAVE A GOOD MEMORY and can recall things with a fair amount of accuracy, but then, I suppose, so do most people. I believe, however, my recollections are correct when I say that none of the people, including myself, who worked on the original *The Little Shop of Horrors* had any idea that it would become a cult film. We were at the time just a bunch of young people, playing around, playing for laughs.

I had made a picture called *A Bucket of Blood* which was a comedy-horror picture that I'd shot in five days. One afternoon, I was having lunch with the manager of what I believe is now called Raleigh Studios. Another film company had just finished shooting and had left behind a nice, rather large set. I wanted to make another comedy-horror picture, only this time I wanted to shoot it in two days. So I told the manager that I'd rent the set for a couple of days if he'd leave it standing. When he agreed, I called a writer friend of mine, Chuck Griffith, and we developed the story as we drifted from one restaurant to another. Which was pretty much the way we'd written *A Bucket of Blood*.

At the time we made *Little Shop*, it cost as much to hire an actor for five days as it did for two days, so I rehearsed the actors for three days and shot them for two, using multiple cameras. On the first day, after shooting for only an hour, the assistant director announced that we were hopelessly behind schedule. Then John Shaner and Jackie Haze did a scene in a dentist's office during which they accidentally knocked over a chair. Dick Rubin, who was the property master, said it would take an hour to put the chair back together. I said: "The scene ends with the dentist chair falling over."

When I finished the picture, Bob Towne* said: "Now you have to remember, Roger, making a movie is not like a track meet; it's not how fast you can go." But I thought *Little Shop* turned out rather well. And at a sneak preview, I discovered that it was much funnier than I thought it was. The audience really liked it. That's why I was surprised and a little disappointed at first when it was only

---

*The Oscar-winning writer of *Chinatown* and numerous other Oscar-nominated screenplays, Robert Towne authored his very first script, *The Last Woman on Earth* (1961), for Roger Corman. He also appeared in that film – as well as *Creature From the Haunted Sea* [Corman's comedy-horror follow-up to *Little Shop*] – under the pseudonym Edward Wain.

moderately successful. Even a moderate success is a success, but a moderate success was something you made from a low budget mystery or western; something tried and true. Something as zany as *Little Shop* should either have been a big hit or a flop. Or so I thought.

A few years before the off-Broadway musical version of *The Little Shop of Horrors* began, I was approached by a French producer who wanted to do it as a play in Paris. Not as a musical comedy but as a comedy-horror, which was the way we had done it. But he was never able to raise the money and so when the off-Broadway people came to me with their idea, I really didn't take it very seriously. If I had, I would probably have negotiated a better deal for myself – although my profit participation extended to the movie and everything else so it's been very pleasant. I have nothing but good thoughts about everyone connected with it.

I liked the new picture. Technically, I thought it was very well made. I liked every aspect of it: the music was excellent; the plant was terrific. I saw it with an audience and it got a lot of laughs. I had the feeling, though, that our film may have gotten a few more laughs. I think Mel Welles got more laughs as Mushnik than the actor playing the same part in the big film. But you can't really compare the two because the original cost $30,000 and the new one cost twenty-plus million dollars. It's an entirely different thing. I think audiences might have treated our film with a little more affection simply because they

knew it was a little picture. They were
sympathetic.
**Roger Corman
Beverly Hills, California**

*Dick Miller and Barboura Morris, the
Seymour and Audrey of* A Bucket of Blood.

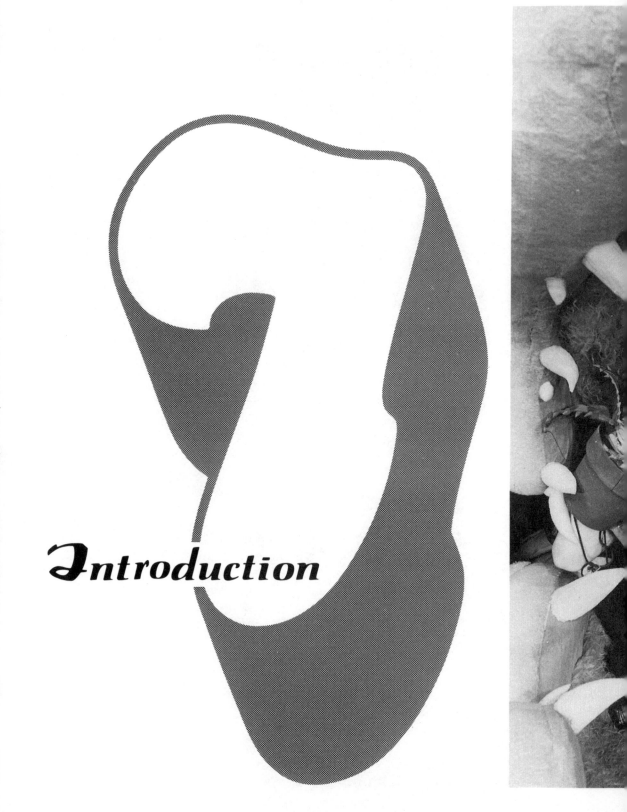

Introduction

Puppeteer Martin P. Robinson poses with three incarnations of his ingenious Audrey II.

SINCE ITS UNHERALDED DEBUT IN 1960, Roger Corman's legendary *The Little Shop of Horrors* has become one of the most popular cult films in movie history. In his book, *Cult Movies*, critic Danny Peary calls it, "the best comedy-horror film around." It has spawned an award-winning off-Broadway musical that has been a hit not only in this country, but in every other land that it has played. And it has resulted in a multi-million dollar movie adaptation of the musical that seems destined for cult status itself. Who would have thought such a thing possible? Certainly not producer-director Roger Corman, who has this to say about his and everybody else's favorite *mad plant movie**:

"The original *Little Shop* was a joke. I was trying to break a record for making a movie ... [yet], in the long run, [this movie] is the one that established me as an underground legend in film circles. [It] had no budget to speak of, yet it has made me more fans and friends than some of my bigger pictures. People come up to me on the street who have memorized parts of the dialogue. I suppose you could say that it was *The Rocky Horror Picture Show* of its time." Even today, Corman feels the film stands up very well, adding: "I can't think of any film that has given

---

**The Films of Roger Corman* by Ed Naha (New York: Arco Publishing, Inc., 1982), page 142.

[me] a better return on investment."

The experience of seeing the original *Little Shop* for the first time is one that people seldom forget. Though it was released to theaters, its fame really spread on television, where it has been a programming staple on late night horror movie shows since the sixties. Most people who recall the film with fondness – including Howard Ashman, who would transfer it to the stage and give it an undreamed of new life – admit to having stumbled upon it by fortunate accident. And that includes ourselves.

Co-author McCarty: "The year was 1965. I was in my junior year as a film student at Boston University. My roommates and I were gathered about the communal television set in our apartment on Friday night, all set to watch "Creature Features," Channel 7's weekly excursion into the land of grade B Hollywood monsterdom. The feature that night was *The Little Shop of Horrors*. None of us had ever heard of it and figured it was a straight horror film – "Creature Features" didn't show comedies, at least not intentional ones. As the film began to unreel, however, we found ourselves laughing hysterically – not *at* the film, but *with* it. And what started out as a typical, collegiate "What do we do with ourselves?" Friday evening turned rapidly into a "happening" that none of us who were there has ever forgotten. We've all seen the film countless times since. And even today, there's not one of us who ever passes up the opportunity to mimic one of Audrey's most amusing mala-

propisms by ordering a "Caesarian" salad when we're out at a restaurant."

Co-author McGee: "I was twelve when I saw *The Little Shop of Horrors.* It was on a double bill at a drive-in with *Black Sunday,* which was the main movie and the one I really wanted to see. I can still remember opening the newspaper and seeing this huge ad for it – two black, penetrating eyes staring back at me from the page. I had high hopes for *Black Sunday* and expected nothing from its companion feature, which didn't rate more than a one column, four line mention. A less interested reader wouldn't have seen it. I may have only been twelve, but I was savvy enough to know a small ad meant even the exhibitors didn't hold much hope for the picture, so neither did I. I ended up having a great time with *Little Shop.* I slept through the other movie."

Our experiences are not unusual. And essentially, that's how *Little Shop*'s cult status grew. People stumbled onto it, told others about it ("Ya gotta see this crazy movie!") and, before long, a cult had developed.

The object of the book you now hold in your hands is to show how this phenomenon occurred and how it has grown and grown over the years like – as Gravis Mushnik would say – "a cold sore from the lip."

The first part of the book concentrates on the original film, revealing

Sadistic dentist Steve Martin meets his match with masochistic patient Bill Murray.

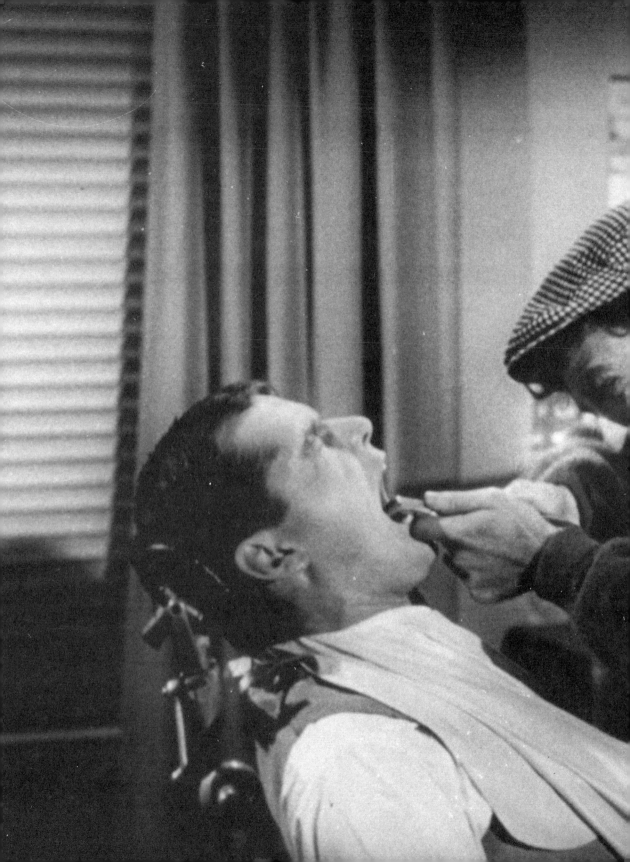

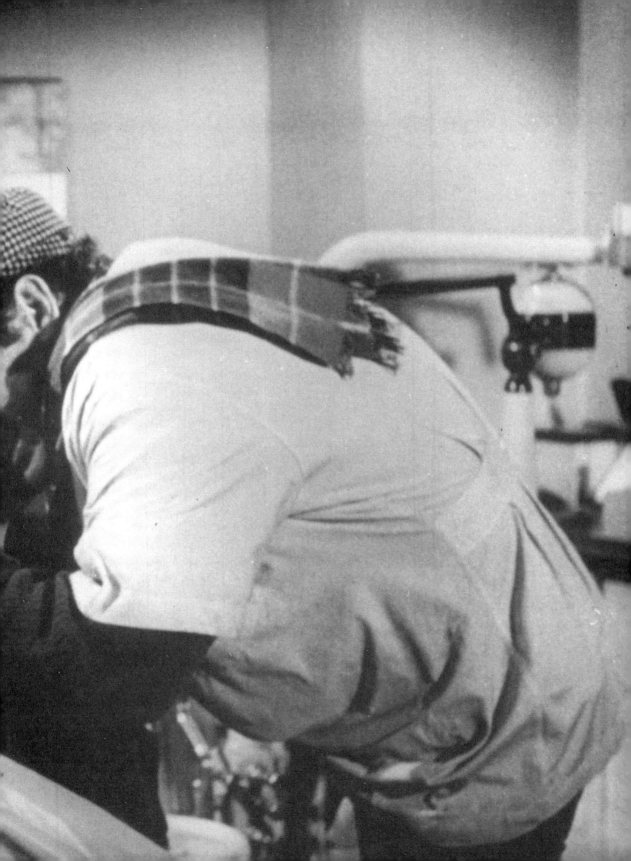

the many funny details behind its making as recounted by some of the main creative talents involved, including: producer-director Corman (in his graciously provided foreword to our book); writer Charles B. Griffith; and stars Jonathan Haze, Jackie Joseph, Mel Welles and Dick Miller. These interviews extend beyond the scope of *Little Shop* itself. That's intentional, for we wanted to give you a real flavor for the backgrounds and personalities of these very inventive and highly talented people as well as an oral history of what low budget moviemaking (for Roger Corman and others) was like back then. *Little Shop* did not emerge out of a vacuum. It was preceded by Corman's *A Bucket of Blood* and followed by *Creature From the Haunted Sea*, two other quickly made horror-comedies which, together with *Little Shop*, form a sort of wacked-out trilogy. Corman would return to the form a scant three years later in 1963 to make *The Raven*, a send-up of his Edgar Allen Poe films starring Boris Karloff, Vincent Price, Peter Lorre and Jack Nicholson. None of these early films had budgets to speak of, yet together they generate more laughs than a dozen big-budget comedies combined. They were made the way Mickey Rooney and Judy Garland used to throw together a musical extravaganza – "Hey, everybody, let's put on a show!". That kind of impromptu moviemaking no longer

exists in today's Hollywood – not even for Roger Corman. The experience of *Little Shop* is therefore unique and will most likely never happen again – certainly not for the same, nor even a comparable, amount of money and effort. [Eegads! To make his own *Little Shop* today, Frank Oz had to spend in excess of $20 million – and filming, plus special effects, took a year!]

Parts two and three focus on the sometimes equally amusing stories, and exceptional talents, behind the creation of the off-Broadway musical and the spectacular Frank Oz movie starring Rick Moranis and Steve Martin which has served to generate even more fame and fortune for the *Little Shop* mythos.

In addition to stage and screen, the bizarre tale of Seymour, Audrey and the latter's carnivorous namesake has also found its way into a variety of other media, in a variety of formats – from records and books to videos and comic books. As an addendum, we've provided a checklist of these items, what they offer, and who offers them.

So, sit back, relax and repeat the magic words. "*Feeeeed Me!*"

Here comes *The Little Shop of Horrors Book.*

Enjoy!

John McCarty
Mark Thomas McGee
August, 1987

Courtesy Mark Thomas McGee Collection

"Oh! My God! Don't stop now!"

The Little Shop of Horrors Book

The Original Film

An ad slick for the original The Little Shop of Horrors.

Background

ON DECEMBER 22, 1959, A MINOR miracle was in the works in Hollywood, a town in urgent need of miracles. This particular one was happening at Amco Studios on La Brea, just below Sunset Drive, the

Funniest film of the year!

old Chaplin Studios. On stage two, the Filmgroup was making a black and white horror-comedy. And the odds against the thing being any good were tremendous. The script had been written in two weeks. The plot had been lifted from another movie. It was being shot in two days and four nights for $36,000. The director was more interested in how quickly he could make it than how well. And one way to shoot it fast was

to film with two cameras running simultaneously. Of course, that meant the lighting would have to be flat and uninteresting, and the composition of the shots would suffer terribly, but how else could you possibly shoot 93 camera set-ups in two days? Taking everything into consideration, the outlook for entertainment was truly bleak. But December is a month of miracles and while the movie that came to be known as *The*

The Cast

Seymour Krelboined	JONATHAN HAZE
Audrey Fulquard	JACKIE JOSEPH
Gravis Mushnik	MEL WELLES
Burson Fouch	DICK MILLER
Winifred Krelboined	MYRTLE VALE
Siddie Shiva	LEOLA WENDORFF
Wilbur Force	JACK NICHOLSON
Phoebus Farb	JOHN SHANER
Leonora Clyde	MERI WELLES
Joe Fink	WALLY CAMPO
Frank Stoolie	JACK WARFORD
Mrs. Fishtwanger	LYNN STOREY
Teenage Girls	TOBY MICHAELS, TAMMY WINDSOR
Waitress	DODIE DRAKE
Kloy Haddock	CHARLES B. GRIFFITH
Drunk	JACK GRIFFITH
Tramp	BOB COOGAR
Voice of Audrey Jr.	CHARLES B. GRIFFITH

The Credits

Producer/Director	ROGER CORMAN
Screenplay	CHARLES B. GRIFFITH
Art Director	DANIEL HALLER
Director of Photography	ARCHIE DALZELL
Second Unit Photography	VILIS LAPENIEKS
Editor	MARSHALL NEILAN
Music	FRED KATZ
Second Unit Direction	CHARLES B. GRIFFITH
Sound Recording	PHILLIP MITCHELL
Makeup	HARRY THOMAS
Property Master	CARL BRAINARD
Assistant Director	RICHARD DIXON

Running Time: 70 minutes

Black and White

Released: April 21, 1961

FILMGROUP

Little Shop of Horrors couldn't exactly be ranked alongside *Citizen Kane*, it *is* a cult classic, one that's survived a quarter of a century, long enough to inspire an off-Broadway musical and a multi-million dollar musical movie remake. Pretty miraculous, all that!

It was Saturday. Roger Corman, an energetic young producer-director, was all psyched up for a game of tennis when it started to rain. "Well," said Corman despondently, "I guess I'll have to make a movie then." And *that* movie turned out to be ... you guessed it. That's one version of the story. Another account has Corman lunching with a business associate who was either his brother [Gene Corman] or the head of Producers Studio or of Amco Studios. And this person, whoever he was, told Corman about a standing set. Corman made a deal to rent the set for two days. Having already made a couple of features in five days, Corman wanted to see if he could make one in two. In a variation on this story, Corman bet his friend that he could make a movie in two days.

A completely different story is told by the author of the original *Little Shop*, Charles Byron Griffith. According to Griffith, the idea evolved while he and Corman were making another

Seymour watches helplessly as a train makes hash of the man [Coogan] he accidentally hit with a rock.

horror-comedy called *A Bucket of Blood*. The cast and crew applauded the first take. Corman was so excited that somebody actually *liked* something for a change that he told Griffith to write another horror-comedy right away, using the same plot.

The plots of *A Bucket of Blood* and *Little Shop* are identical. The heroes are well-meaning schlepps who inadvertently become murderers. Their crimes ultimately bring them fame and fortune, but to remain successful, they must keep on killing. When the truth is finally revealed, they commit suicide.

In *Little Shop*, the hero is Seymour Krelboined, a go-fer for Gravis Mushnik, the owner of a skid-row flower shop. Seymour is about to lose his job when the boss sees the new species of plant Seymour cultivated by crossing a Venus Fly-Trap with a buttercup. Mushnik is convinced that Seymour's plant will attract business, so Seymour's job is saved if he can only keep the thing alive. Unfortunately, the only way he can do that is by supplying the plant with the only thing it will eat ... *people.*

Griffith's original title was *The Passionate People-Eater*. While he was writing the script, Corman had Dice Incorporated busy bringing Griffith's people-eating plant to life. Dice specialized in "decorative props." For one of Corman's earlier films, they'd built a 25 ft. crab. The prop had not been very decorative and had incited laughter from small children.

At least *Little Shop* was *supposed* to be funny.

On December 21, the day before production, Dice delivered a four inch, a twelve inch, a six foot, and an eight foot plant to Corman's office on Amco's lot. Some normal looking plastic leaves and plants were included in the shipment together with some art work. All of this for a modest $750.00. By that time, Griffith had completed two drafts of the script for which he received $800.00.

At 7:45 the following morning, Corman ordered his cameras to roll and by 9:15 in the evening of the next day, he'd finished the bulk of the picture. Griffith, actors Mel Welles and Jonathan Haze, and photographer Vilis Lapenieks supplied what was left, around fifteen minutes, for $1,100.00. And for a mere $317.34, Fred Katz gave the film its musical score. In keeping with the spirit of the project, Katz simply used the same score he'd written for *A Bucket of Blood*, which had also been used in another Corman film, *The Wasp Woman* and would be used yet again in Corman's *Creature From the Haunted Sea*. Whether or not Corman was aware he was buying the same score three times is unknown.

When the picture was finished, Corman flew to Puerto Rico and raced through two more movies, *Creature From the Haunted Sea* (another horror-comedy written by Chuck Griffith) and *The Last Woman on Earth* (a serious end-of-the-world drama written by Robert Towne). The latter film he packaged with *Little Shop* and offered to the exhibitors in the fall of 1960. But they didn't want *Little Shop*, not because it was cheap and cheesy, but because they thought it was *anti-Semitic*!

In both *Little Shop* and *A Bucket of Blood*, there's a character who knows the hero is a murderer but keeps quiet because of the profit he stands to make. In *Bucket*, the character is Italian. In *Little Shop*, he's Jewish. And that made the film anti-Semitic as far as the exhibitors were concerned, so the picture was shelved. Then American-International, looking for a second feature to package with a horror film it had imported from Italy, agreed to take *Little Shop*. The import (*Black Sunday*) was top-lining the program. The second feature was just for dressing. Anything would do. Even something "anti-Semitic".

But the critics didn't find the film anti-Semitic. In fact, the response, what little there was, was favorable. *Motion Picture Herald*, a trade publication, liked it. *Variety* called it lowbrow comedy, but had to admit it was funny. "In short," wrote the reviewer, "the film is a sort of rowdy vegetable that hits the funnybone in about the same way that seeing a man slip on a banana peel does. It's absurd."

Mel Welles took those reviews to the officials at Cannes, who immediately wired Corman for a print. Corman had already withdrawn the film from general release in the hope that he could get a better play out of it in art houses. A screening at the Cannes Film Festival could only increase those chances.

There were only two U.S. films in official competition at the festival that year, Columbia's *A Raisin in the Sun* with Sidney Poitier and United Artists' *The Hoodlum Priest* with Don Murray. There were, however, two more films on the unofficial list: Otto Preminger's film version of Leon Uris' best-seller *Exodus* and Roger Corman's *The Little Shop of Horrors*. Yet, in spite of the showing at Cannes, the picture came and went without causing a ripple. Corman got his usual six-month run out of the picture and then retired it without bothering to copyright it. It wasn't until the mid-sixties, when it was sold to Allied Artists for television release, that people started taking notice of it.

Not long after that the film was revived by theaters catering to college audiences. It became (as Corman suggested) *The Rocky Horror Picture Show* of its time. Now, because

Courtesy Mark Thomas McGee Collection

Jack Nicholson as masochistic dental patient Wilbur Force.

Jonathan Haze photographed on skid row with a concealed camera.

Courtesy Mark Thomas McGee Collection

of the off-Broadway musical and the new movie, the original *Little Shop* is enjoying yet another revival. One videocassette outfit recently released a colorized version. You can buy a bootleg black and white version for ten bucks. There's even a soundtrack album. In all probability, the picture will be around for at least another quarter of a century.

Sometimes, movies are called classics just because they're old. But a real classic is one of those rare films where all the elements are in complete harmony and the story being told is timeless. *The Little Shop of Horrors* may well qualify as a classic if you subscribe to that definition. Which is really the funniest thing about it. The flat lighting, the bare-bones look of the sets, the barely competent photography – things that would work against a normal movie – become part of the charm, the film's poverty part of the joke. It's a counterfeit movie, but it's irresistible. And very funny, too.

But is it a classic? Who knows? Maybe it's an anti-classic. What we *do* know is that it's taken us a lot longer to write this book than it took Roger Corman to make his movie. And that's pretty funny too. But now it's time to unravel the events surrounding this legendary 25-year-old movie that was shot in two days. How many events could there have been? Well, in an effort to find out, the four principal players, plus the film's writer, were interviewed at length; the results are recorded next. [Roger Corman you've already heard from.] Hopefully, from them, you'll learn everything you've ever wanted to know about *The Little Shop of Horrors*, the atmosphere of filmmaking out of which it grew, and the people who were most involved in bringing it to life – a task which, you now realize, was no easy one.

The Story

MUSHNIK'S FLOWERS IS LOCATED IN Los Angeles, California, in a section of the city that everyone knows about but nobody wants to see, where the tragedies are deeper, the ecstasies wilder, and the crime rate consistently higher than anywhere else — skid row. The owner of the shop is Gravis Mushnik, a plump, bearded man given to outbursts of rage, nurtured by the frustration of having to make a living from a ragtag business in the poorest section of town. Mushnik's ancestors have been in the flower business for over two hundred years yet, unhappily, he has been unable to carve a secure niche for himself. Adding to his frustration is the simple fact that he doesn't even like flowers. (Worse still, his name is misspelled on the sign out front because the movie's art director didn't know any better.)

Business being what it is, Mushnik can't afford more than ten dollars a week for a go-fer. For that amount of money the pickings are slim and Mushnik has had to settle

Courtesy Mark Thomas McGee Collection

"You can talk. I've got a talking plant!" exclaims Seymour.

Courtesy Mark Thomas McGee Collection

For these night shots, Charles Griffith paid the local residents 10¢ a shot.

for a clumsy but well-meaning simpleton named Seymour Krelboined (or Krelboin depending on where you get your information). Seymour's constant bungling makes him an easy target for Mushnik's anger. (He once got his orders switched and sent black lilies to an old lady in a hospital while the bouquet with the get well card that should have gone to her was delivered to a funeral parlor.)

And Seymour is in love with Audrey Fulquard, Mushnik's dark-haired, addle-brained but sweet young assistant who has a penchant for malapropisms. Unbeknownst to

Seymour, Audrey thinks he's a fine "figurative" of a man.

The first customer of the day is Siddie Shiva, a dried-up old prune of a woman who has a seemingly endless supply of relatives who kick off on an almost daily basis. She treats each one as if it were the first, entering the shop on the verge of tears, chastising anyone present who doesn't appear to share her grief. On this particular morning she's making like a banshee over the passing of her sister's nephew, Stanley, in Little Rock, Arkansas. Eyeing some roses, she pauses in her caterwauling long

Courtesy Mark Thomas McGee Collection

Audrey Junior, waiting for its next meal.

enough to ask Mushnik for a cut rate, seeing as how she gives him all of her business, which is considerable indeed.

"Look on me, Mrs. Shiva," Mushnik says respectfully. "What am I, a philatolist? I sell on skid row nothing but cheap carnations. And I should give you a cut rate? I can't even afford water for the flowers. To my throat I would be giving a cut."

That settled, Mushnik takes a call from Dr. Phoebus Farb, a sadistic skid row dentist and another regular customer. Unfortunately, Farb's business is little better than Mushnik's

and his flower budget for the week permits nothing more than two gladioli and a fern. Mushnik hangs up and yells for Seymour. Seymour races from the backroom, steps into a bucket, loses his balance, and stumbles into Mushnik.

"You called me, Mr. Mushnik," Seymour says with a forced smile.

"No," Mushnik says sarcastically. "I was calling John D. Rockefeller for to make a loan on my Rolls-Royce!"

Calming himself, Mushnik explains to Seymour what he needs: two gladioli trimmed to equal length and a fern. It's a simple task but one that proves

Courtesy Mark Thomas McGee Collection

Feeeeeeeed meeeeeeeee," cries Junior.

too much for Seymour. He ends up butchering the two gladioli and Mushnik is forced to watch in perplexed silence while he waits on another customer, a short, dark man in a yellow vest. His name is Burson Fouch and he orders two dozen carnations. Flowers-fresh-as-the-springtime Mushnik offers to wrap them but Fouch says, "That's all right. I'll eat 'em here." Fouch has eaten in flower shops all over the world, preferring little out-of-the-way places like Mushnik's to the fancier shops. Those places might have prettier, more expensive flowers but flowers raised for looks and smell lose food value. Fouch pulls a salt shaker from his pocket, lightly sprinkles his carnations and chows down.

Still recovering from the shock of seeing his new customer eating flowers, Mushnik now has time to deal with Seymour. Displaying what's left of the two gladioli, Mushnik bellows: "Look on him, everyone. Look at the quality of his work. I ask you, when I fire him, where is he gonna get such another good job?"

Taken aback, Seymour says, "You mean ... I'm fired?"

"No. I'm electing you president from the United States. YES! YOU ARE FIRED!"

Audrey steps in on Seymour's behalf and suggests that Mushnik give him a chance to "resurrect himself."

"I'll give him a chance to quit," Mushnik snaps.

"I ain't gonna quit."

"You're a brave boy. You're fired."

"But that ain't fair, Mr. Mushnik.

I'm working on a surprise plant, just for you. I'm growing a plant like you ain't never seen before."

Mushnik's not interested in another plant. He can't even sell what he's already got. He's all set to toss Seymour out on his ear when the man in the yellow vest tells Mushnik he may be making a serious mistake. Speaking with some authority, Fouch claims that the flower shops with the most unusual plants do the best business. "I know one place," he recalls, "that had a whole wall covered with poison ivy. The people came from miles around to look at that wall and they stayed to buy."

"And the owner got rich?" Mushnik asks, suddenly interested.

"No. He scratched himself to death in an insane asylum."

"Oh!" gasps Mrs. Shiva. "That was my cousin, Harry."

Mushnik is not convinced. He wants Fouch to see Seymour's plant before a final decision is made. It turns out to be a sickly-looking egg-shaped thing, grown from seeds he got from a Japanese farmer on Central Avenue who got them from a plantation next to a cranberry farm.

"Fine. Fine. You don't even know what is this plant you are growing," Mushnik notes.

"Well," Seymour adds, "I gave it a name."

You gotta be kidding! We're gonna make this movie in two days! From The Little Shop of Horrors.

"What name?" Audrey asks.
But Seymour is reluctant to say.
"What?" Mushnik barks, jumping to conclusions. "You gave it a dirty name? You can't even mention it?"
"I named it

"Oh fine. In this fancy shmancy restaurant you are holding hostages, right?" bellows *Mushnik.*

Courtesy Mark Thomas McGee Collection

Audrey Junior."
Audrey is thrilled. It's the most
exciting thing anyone ever did for her.

But Mushnik is still not convinced that Seymour is worth $10 a week.

"But Gravis," Audrey bubbles, "he named it after me."

"I know, and if I keep it they'll name it Mushnik's folly because I'll be in jail for non-payment of taxes."

"Are you crazy?" Fouch says. "That's probably the only plant of its kind in the world. Don't you realize if Seymour can nurse that thing back to health you'll have people coming here from all over."

Hoping that Fouch is right, Mushnik gives Seymour one week to get the plant into shape. Audrey is delighted but Seymour's not so sure he can do it having already given the thing every kind of fancy fertilizer, atomic plant food, and distilled mineral water he could buy.

"Don't feel bad, Seymour," Audrey tells him.

"Don't waste your pity on me, Audrey. I'm not worth it."

"Who says you're not?"

"Everybody."

"Yeah. I know. You're gonna be another Luther Glendale."

"Pasadena."

"Burbank."

That night, alone in the shop, quite by accident, Seymour discovers the horrible truth about Audrey Junior. Pricking his finger on one of the other plants, Seymour shakes his finger in pain. A few drops fall on Junior. The plant opens like a happy clam. Repulsed, Seymour squeezes a few more drops from his finger. Junior laps them up.

The next morning Seymour returns to Mushnik's with ten bandaged fingers. Mushnik and Audrey are waiting for him with smiling faces. The plant has doubled in size — it's nearly a foot long. Already Mushnik is making plans to move to Beverly Hills and build a giant greenhouse for Seymour to grow impossible flowers in, which Mushnik will sell at ridiculous prices in his giant flower "saloon." Gravis Mushnik, the "Bloom Tycoon." No longer does he want Seymour to call him Mister Mushnik. "I want you should call me Dad."

Two teenaged girls drop into the shop, ostensibly to have a look at Junior. And while they're looking they happen to mention they have $2000 to spend on flowers for their school float which is to be entered in the Rose Bowl Parade.

"Tell me," says Mushnik, "how come you don't buy all these thousands of flowers from Gravis Mushnik. My flowers got something the others don't."

"What's that?" asks one of the girls.

Courtesy Mark Thomas McGee Collection

Bobbie Coogan, playing an undercover policeman, is about to be bonked on the head.

"They're cheap," Seymour volunteers.

After thinking it over the girls decide that any shop good enough to develop the Audrey Junior is good enough for them. The moment they're out of the door Mushnik is back in fantasyland. He envisions a giant sign in the sky. It reads: Gravis Mushnik. In French. He's in a state of high hilarity by the time that Siddie Shiva drops in for her daily ration of flowers. She, of course, can't imagine how anyone can be happy when her uncle's brother just passed away in New Jersey. Without a second's thought, Mushnik gives her a couple of dozen carnations ... on the house. On the way out Siddie tells Mushnik he ought to give some flowers "to that poor dead plant there."

Mushnik, Seymour and Audrey look to see what plant Siddie is referring to and to their mutual horror and surprise it's Junior. "Look what happened to my

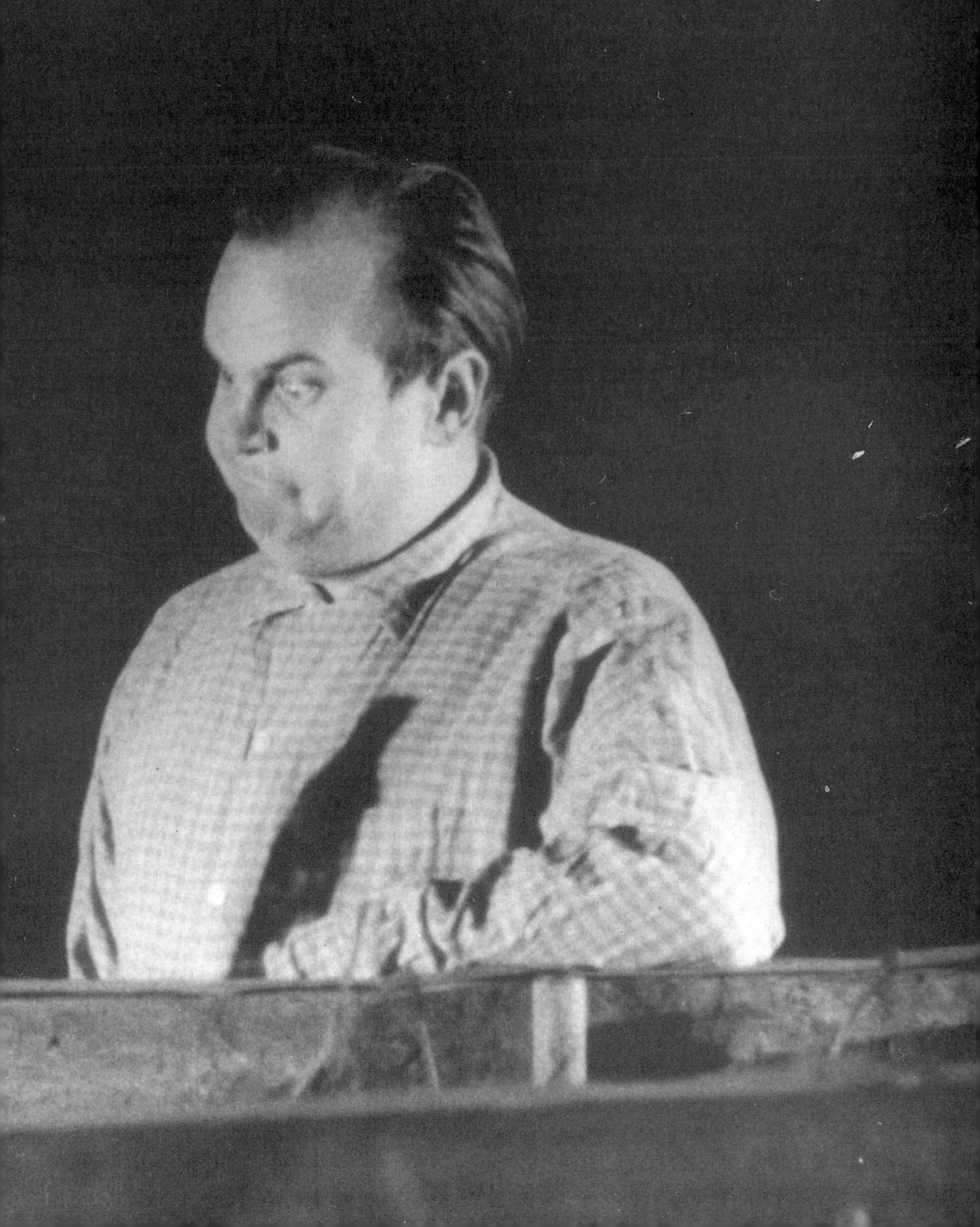

plant, Dad," Seymour groans.

"Who you calling Dad? Who? Who?"

Only a few seconds before Mushnik saw himself in Beverly Hills with his name in French on a gargantuan sign. Now he's back on skid row and the big sign has been replaced by one that reads: Seymour Krelboined – Rest in Peace. In Arabic!

Seymour promises that by morning the plant will be healthy again.

That night, as he wonders what to do about Junior, Seymour is shocked to learn that he's bred a talking plant. And when it speaks, it's got one thing on its mind – food. But Seymour's pretty well exhausted the supply in his fingers so he wanders into the night, hoping he can figure out a way to feed his creation. He ends up in the freight yard, idly pitching rocks at an old bottle. As a particularly large rock leaves his hand a man suddenly appears next to the bottle. The rock hits him on the head, knocking him senseless. Before Seymour's horrified eyes the poor fool staggers onto the tracks where he is hit by a passing train.* Afraid and confused, Seymour gathers the pieces of the corpse, puts

---

*Mel Welles, the actor who played Gravis Mushnik, told Dennis Fisher, in *Cinefantastique* magazine, how this scene was accomplished: "I got the Southern Pacific Railway yard, a train, and a crew to drive it. They backed it up so that when it was printed in reverse, it looked like Bobbie Coogan [the actor playing the railroad detective] was hit." Welles considered this whole sequence his *coup de grace* since the whole bit cost a measly two bottles of Scotch. That same day 20th Century-Fox had paid $15,000 for the use of the same location.

them in a bag, and returns to the shop, where he gets little sympathy from Junior. Junior is still waiting for dinner.

"Do you think it's fun to be a murderer?" Seymour asks him. "Do you think it's fun to haul around a sack full of ..."

"Food!" Junior intones.

"Oh no, Junior. What kind of a guy do you think I am?"

"I'm *starved*!"

Meanwhile, Mushnik and Audrey are dining at one of the local dives when Mushnik discovers that he's left his wallet in his other suit. He goes back to the shop to get some money from the register and sees Seymour feeding body parts to the plant. Mushnik falls into a mild state of shock. The next morning he intends to call the police. But there's a crowd gathered outside of his shop and there are even more people crowded inside. Business is booming and it's all because of Seymour's people-eating plant, which has quadrupled in size. Mushnik drags Seymour into the back room and demands to know more about the plant. Seymour explains that it's a cross between a buttercup and a Venus's-flytrap. According to the books, a flytrap only eats three times before it's full grown. Seymour can't remember how many meals Junior's had but he's convinced it can't get any bigger and Mushnik wants to believe him. Se he sends Seymour off to the dentist to take care of his bad tooth.

Like most of Seymour's experiences, the trip to Dr. Farb ends miserably. Farb insists on removing more than just the bad tooth and he and Seymour get into a fight during which Farb is stabbed to death with his own drill. Seymour hides the body and is forced to impersonate the doctor when a new patient insists on being treated. The patient's name is Wilbur Force, a mortician who enjoys pain. No Novacaine for him. And when it's all over, Wilbur confesses that he's never had such a good time and promises to recommend Seymour to all of his friends.

Seymour carries Farb's body back to the shop and feeds it to Junior.

It's quite possible that the disappearance of the man in the railroad yard would have gone unnoticed if he hadn't been a detective. Sergeant Joe Fink is asked to investigate. He summons his partner, Frank Stoolie.

"How's the wife, Frank?"

"Not bad, Joe."

"Glad to hear it. Kids?"

"Lost one yesterday."

"Lost one, eh? How'd that happen?"

"Playing with matches."

"Well, those are the breaks."

"Yeah. I guess so."

More distressed is Gravis Mushnik when he sees that Junior has grown again. Seymour tells him Junior ate about a million Japanese beetles and has eaten for the last time but Mushnik isn't convinced. He decides to babysit the plant.

That night, on cue, Junior opens up and asks for supper. At first, Mushnik is taken aback by the fact that Junior can talk but the surprise quickly turns to anger.

"Who would you like to have tonight?" Mushnik asks in outrage.

"You look fat enough," Junior replies.

"We not only got a talking plant," observes Mushnik, "we got one that makes with smart cracks. Well, you listen to me you botanical bum, food you wouldn't get. Not from Gravis Mushnik."

"I'm *starved*."

"Excellent. You would un-populate all skid row. Well, you can forget about it."

But, as Seymour could have told Mushnik, the best of intentions are often thwarted by circumstance. A thief breaks into the shop and, at gun point, demands money. Mushnik empties the register but the miserable thirty bucks he hands the crook isn't enough. He'd been in the shop earlier that day and had seen all of the people and even though Mushnik tells him that most of those people simply dropped in to look at the plant, the crook is certain that Mushnik is holding out on him. With the business end of a gun staring him in the face, Mushnik tells the crook that the rest of the money is hidden in the plant.

"How do you get it open?" the crook asks.

"Just knock," Mushnik replies.

The crook knocks, Junior opens, the crook reaches inside and Junior gobbles him up.

As the plant grows, so does its reputation. A pinchbutt woman from The Society of Silent Flower Observers of Southern California — Hortense Fishtwanger — announces her intention to give Seymour the Society's

annual trophy.

"Tell me, Mr. Krelboined," Mrs. Fishtwanger says, "is this a freak or can more be raised from the seeds?"

"We should live so long," Mushnik mutters to himself.

"I think this is gonna be the only one," Seymour tells her.

"It's probably indigestible anyway," Burson Fouch adds.

"When do you suppose those large buds will open?" Mrs. Fishtwanger asks.

"Well, according to what the book

Courtesy Mark Thomas McGee Collection

"Get me whisky, rum, wine, gin, bourbon, scotch, tequila, Maneshewitz!" cries Mushnik.

says about the plants that I crossed, they should open day after tomorrow at sunset."

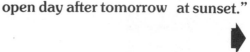

Courtesy Mark Thomas McGee Collection

Junior's first substantial meal – the remains of the undercover policeman.

Courtesy Mark Thomas McGee Collection

Mushnik sees Seymour feeding body parts to the plant.

Mrs. Fishtwanger says that she'll return at that time to present the trophy.

But the price for all of this fame seems too high to Seymour. He refuses Junior's next request for food, so Junior hypnotises him. "You will go and find me some food," the plant commands and Seymour obeys. A blonde hooker named Leonora Clyde becomes Junior's next meal.*

---

*This sequence was a last minute addition to replace a sequence in the script where Seymour is haunted by the people he'd murdered. The substitution was made for budgetary reasons. The hooker was played by Meri Welles, Mel's wife.

The following evening, at sunset, Mushnik's is filled with people who've come to watch Seymour get his award. Joe Fink and Frank Stoolie are among the people in the crowd. Frank tells Seymour's mother they're still investigating the rash of disappearances on skid row. "We think they were murdered," he says.

"Look here, young man," Mrs. Krelboined says, "that's no way to

Courtesy Mark Thomas McGee Collection

Mushnik has never seen his shop so full. Burson Fouch wants to know if he'll sell him half an interest in the business.

talk at a time like this. Let me see your tongue. Know what you got?"

"Just the facts, ma'am."

"Trench mouth."

"Better have that looked into, Frank," Joe remarks.

"Whatever you say, Joe."

As the sun sets, the buds open, each containing the face of one of Junior's victims. The two policemen chase Seymour from the shop but he manages to elude them. Later, Seymour attempts to destroy his creation but ends up its victim instead, just another face on one of the buds.

The girls want to use Audrey Junior as part of their high school float. They want their queen to sit inside it.

The Interviews

JONATHAN HAZE
as Seymour Krelboined

JONATHAN (OR "JACKIE" TO HIS friends) Haze has the distinction of being the very first member of what came to be the Roger Corman Stock Company Players. Because of the short shooting schedules of Corman's films, the performers had to know their lines, hit their marks, and give a believable accounting of themselves with little or no rehearsal. For six years, Jonathan Haze worked with Corman as an actor, dialogue coach and stunt co-ordinator.

"That was something you have to give Roger a lot of credit for," Haze remarked. "If you told him you could do something, he'd let you do it. If you came in with a certain way to play a part, he'd tell you to go ahead. It didn't always work out, but most of the time it did."

Haze was born on April 1, 1929, in Pittsburgh, Pennsylvania. His father was in the jewelry business and was able to keep food on the table. He wanted his son to be a jockey but Jonathan grew too tall and wasn't interested in horse racing anyway. He'd set his sights on show business, having been influenced by his cousin, the late Buddy Rich, who was one of the all-time great jazz drummers. Rich played with Harry James, Tommy Dorsey, Artie Shaw, people like that. When Rich played the Stanley Theater

in Pittsburgh, Jonathan would always go backstage. The excitement crept into his soul and overtook him. He decided to go to New York to do summer stock.

"I was living in a hotel room for something like fifteen bucks a week," Haze recalled. "There were a lot of young people. Things were cheap. It was exciting. It was life. There was music all night and people were out there having a good time."

He worked as an apprentice for the Norwich Summer Theater in Connecticut, then returned to New York looking for work as an actor. That didn't work out so he went on tour with Buddy. He was Josephine Baker's stage manager for a while and also worked with the Civic Light Opera. In the early fifties he came to California to take a shot at the movies. He pumped gas at night to pay bills, and auditioned during the day. Now and then a little guy in a beat up old car came into the station. His name was Barney Ordung and he claimed he was going to make a movie with a guy named Roger Corman.

"In those days everybody in Hollywood was going to make a picture," Jonathan remarked. "You didn't really think that much about it."

It was Ordung that introduced Jonathan to Roger Corman, who gave Jonathan a part in a little something called *Monster From the Ocean Floor*

Courtesy Mark Thomas McGee Collection

"You gave this plant a fancy name, but I want to know what do just plain people call it?" Mushnik asks Seymour.

Seymour is about to botch another job as his boss, Gravis Mushnik, looks on.

which Ordung directed. Jonathan continued to appear in Corman films on a regular basis for the next six years. At the time, *The Little Shop of Horrors* was just another of those films. It has since become Jonathan's favorite.

HAZE: It's the one everybody remembers me for. At the time it was just another job, just another Corman film. There was nothing special about it. That didn't happen until much later. Now I'm invited to conventions and people ask me questions about it —which is nice and everything, but I can't take any of it seriously. It's really hard for me to even remember working on it, you know, it was such a long time ago. It's another lifetime. I went through a period in my life where I tried to forget all that so I don't really remember a lot about those days. I wanted to forget it and get on with my life.

Q: Why?

HAZE: I'd gotten depressed with the business.

Q: When was this?

HAZE: It was right after *Little Shop*

or soon after. I wanted to write a comedy for Dick [Miller] and me to star in. Roger wanted us to write it together. And we did that for a while until I just couldn't do it anymore. Dick wanted to worry over each line until it was perfect, which is all right if you can work that way, but I can't. I like to go straight through and *then* go back and do the rewriting. So I said to Dick, "Look, I can't write this way. Let me just write it down and then you can rewrite it." Well, he didn't like that and he told Roger he didn't want to do the picture. So Roger changed his mind about making it and wouldn't pay me the $1500 for the script. So I took it to Jim Nicholson because I'd used the names of the people that worked at [American International] in the script. It was called *The Monsters of Nicholson Mesa* then. Nicholson loved it. And he was ready to buy it but Roger told him, "He's asking for more money than I was going to pay him. Just hold on. I can get it for less." So the thing sat in my drawer for over a year. Then Mel Welles was forming his own company with a guy named Berg Hajkopian and they needed a script so they bought this script and then the company went bankrupt. The script fell into AIP's hands somehow and they changed the title to *Invasion of the Star Creatures*. At the time I didn't even know it was being made. I never saw it until years later when it turned up on television. It was really crappy. That really turned me off of the business for a while, that whole experience.

Q: Why did Roger do that to you?

HAZE: I don't know. I don't think it was anything personal. We weren't getting along that well but I don't think that had anything to do with it. I think it was just business.

Q: If you and Roger weren't on friendly terms, why did he choose you for the lead of *The Little Shop*?

HAZE: That part had been written for Dick Miller but Dick didn't want to do it because it was just like what he'd done in *A Bucket of Blood*. It was the same character. I guess I was the only one else around who could do it. So Roger offered it to me and I needed the money so I took it. It was a job.

Q: Did you study acting?

HAZE: I took a few classes when I came to California but nothing serious. I thought I could do it without learning it, you know. In those days it was *doing* that counted. The experience was what was important. I still feel that way. It's more important to do something for the experience than it is to do it for the money.

Q: Did you always want to be an actor?

HAZE: Not really. I just knew I wanted to be in the limelight. And when I was growing up in Pittsburgh there were two ways for young men to make a lot money – as an athlete or as an actor. I did a little boxing in those days but I never thought seriously about making it a profession because in those days there were professional boxers getting as little as fifty bucks a fight.

Q: From what I've heard you

couldn't make a whole lot of money working for Corman.

HAZE: But you gotta remember that it was a lot cheaper to live then. You could get an apartment for fifty bucks a month. Gas was twenty cents. You didn't need a lot of money. And I was more interested in the experience. When you're writing this thing don't make Roger a villain. He gave chances to a lot of people and he was the only one doing it. I got the opportunity to play a lot of different kinds of roles in those pictures. Where else could you play a cowboy one week and a gangster the next? Nobody else was doing anything like that. The part I had in *Not of This Earth*, the sleazy chauffeur ... That was a great part. I don't think there was anyone else who would have let me do a part like that. It was a great experience.

Q: Was Corman much help in directing the perform- ances of the actors?

HAZE: No. It was pretty much every man for himself. Whatever you saw on the screen was what the actor

brought with him. But that was okay because he'd let you do what you wanted.

Q: You didn't just act in those pic- tures, you were also the one who staged the fights.

HAZE: I did a lot of things in those pictures. I drove the race cars in *The Fast and the Furious*.

Q: I didn't know that.

Courtesy Mark Thomas McGee Collection

Dr. Phoebus Farb doesn't believe in using Novacaine, much to Seymour's dismay.

V.W.S.S. 16

one of the cars and in this particular scene the hero was supposed to pass him but Roger wanted to win the race and ruined the take.

HAZE: I don't remember anything like that. Roger may have driven one of the cars but I don't remember. He may have. It was a long time ago. A lot of Roger's friends drove cars in that picture. People did a lot of things for Roger. And sometimes he took advantage. Like when we made *Viking Women and the Sea Serpent.* He had all of these young girls in a boat and the tide came up and took them out to sea. A lot of people took a lot of chances.

Q: You had a pretty big role in that one.

HAZE: Yeah. I had to dye my hair blond. There's a funny story about that. I was supposed to go to this wedding and the day before I went swimming, the chlorine in the water turned my hair green and I had to go to this wedding with green hair.

Q: Dick Miller told me that when you and he were in Hawaii making *Naked Paradise* the two of you used to play practical jokes on Roger.

HAZE: We may have. I don't remember. You know, I don't think a lot about that period of my life. I don't think it does anybody a lot of good to dwell on the past. I used to have scrapbooks and stuff in an old trunk. It

Copyright © 1958 American International Pictures

Richard Devon and Jonathan Haze have a squabble while Abby Dalton, June Kenney and Susan Cabot look on. From Viking Women and the Sea Serpent.

Maybe you could confirm a story I heard about that picture. Roger said *he* was driving rained and the stuff got ruined. I would like to have had some of those things but I'm not broken up about it.

Q: Did you ever work for anybody besides Corman?

HAZE: Oh, sure. I did a lot of *Divorce Courts* and *Highway Patrols.* TV. And I played a part in *East of Eden* but most of what I did was cut out.

Q: Why?

HAZE: I guess because the picture was running too long. There was a whole other story going on that was really never shown [in the final version].

Q: And you were also in *Stakeout on Dope Street.*

HAZE: That's right, but Roger had something to do with that too. He had some money in it.

Q: How do you feel about your performances in those pictures?

HAZE: I think some of them were pretty good. I don't know that I could pick one that I liked better than any other. Maybe *Little Shop,* but maybe that's because people like me in it. Harry Guardino once told me I was his favorite actor because of that picture. I guess I was good in it. But I don't think it's my performance that has made that picture last. And I don't think it's Roger's direction or Chuck's writing or anybody else's acting.

Q: What do you think it was?

HAZE: Who knows? It was different. I think it surprised a lot of people. If it had been a bigger picture – if one of the big studios had made it – I don't think people would have treated it the way they have. It just wouldn't

Neither Jonathan Haze nor Leslie Bradley looks much like a Teenage Caveman.

Copyright © 1958 American International Pictures

have been the same.

Q: Was Roger there when you were shooting the night scenes?

HAZE: No. He had nothing to do with that. That was me and Chuck Griffith and Mel Welles. All that stuff was non-union. We shot all that on skid row. We had all of these bums in the picture for ten cents a shot. They'd save enough to buy a bottle of wine, drink it, and be back for more.

Beverly Garland and Jonathan Haze discover their employer is Not of This Earth.

After *Little Shop,* Haze appeared less frequently in films and eventually found more comfort on the other side of the camera. He's worked as an assistant director, a production manager and a producer. Because of his association with the film *Stakeout on Dope Street* he became friends with the award-winning photographer Haskell Wexler and the two of them often work together.

FILMOGRAPHY
(As Performer)

1954

The Monster From the Ocean Floor
Lippert
Screenplay by William Danch
Produced by Roger Corman
Directed by Wyott Ordung

The Fast and the Furious
American International
Screenplay by Jerome Odlum and Jean Howell
Produced by Roger Corman
Directed by Edward Samson and John Ireland

1955

East of Eden Warner Brothers
Screenplay by Paul Osborn
based on the novel by John Steinbeck
Directed by Elia Kazan

Five Guns West
American Releasing Corporation
Screenplay by R. Wright (Bobby)
Campbell, *Produced and Directed by*
Roger Corman

Cell 2455, Death Row Columbia
Screenplay by Jack De Witt
based on Caryl Chessman's book
Produced by Wallace MacDonald
Directed by Fred F. Sears

Apache Woman
American Releasing Corporation
Screenplay by Lou Rusoff, *Produced
and Directed by* Roger Corman

1956

The Day the World Ended
American Releasing Corporation
Screenplay by Lou Rusoff, *Produced
and Directed by* Roger Corman

The Bold and the Brave
RKO Radio Pictures
Screenplay by Robert Lewin
Produced by Hal E. Chester
Directed by Lewis R. Foster

Swamp Women Woolner Brothers
Screenplay by David Stern
Produced by Bernard Woolner
Directed by Roger Corman

Gunslinger
American Releasing Corporation
Screenplay by Charles B. Griffith,
Mark Hanna, *Produced and Directed
by* Roger Corman

It Conquered the World
American International
Screenplay by Lou Rusoff and
(uncredited) Charles B. Griffith
Produced and Directed by
Roger Corman

1957

Carnival Rock Howco International
Screenplay by Leo Lieberman
Produced and Directed by
Roger Corman

Naked Paradise (a.k.a. **Thunder
Over Hawaii**) American International
Screenplay by Charles B. Griffith,
Mark Hanna and (uncredited)
R. Wright Campbell, *Produced and
Directed by* Roger Corman

Copyright © 1955 American Releasing Corp.

*Jonathan Haze as one of the mutants
created by atomic radiation in* The Day
The World Ended.

Not of This Earth Allied Artists
Screenplay by Charles B. Griffith
and Mark Hanna, *Produced and
Directed by* Roger Corman

Rock All Night
American International
Screenplay by Charles B. Griffith
based on "The Little Guy"
Produced and Directed by
Roger Corman

Bayou (a.k.a. ***Poor White Trash***)
United Artists
Screenplay by Edward L. Femler

Copyright © 1957 American Releasing Corp.

*Jonathan Haze looks on as Russell Johnson
shows Ed Nelson the business end of his
gun. From* Rock All Night.

Produced by M. A. Ripps
Directed by Harold Daniels

Viking Women and the Sea Serpent (a.k.a. ***The Saga of the Viking
Women and Their Voyage to the
Waters of the Great Sea Serpent***)
American International
Screenplay by Lawrence Louis
Goldman, *Produced and Directed by*
Roger Corman

1958

Stakeout on Dope Street
Warner Brothers
Screenplay by Irvin Kirshner,
Irwin Schwartz and Andrew J. Fenady
Produced by Andrew J. Fenady
Directed by Irvin Kershner

Jonathan Haze and Dorothy Malone in Five Guns West.

Teenage Caveman
(a.k.a. *Prehistoric World*)
American International
Screenplay by R. Wright Campbell
Produced and Directed by
Roger Corman

Ghost of the China Sea Columbia
Written, Produced and Directed by
Charles B. Griffith

1963

The Terror Filmgroup/
American International
Screenplay by Leo Gordon and Jack
Hill, *Produced by* Roger Corman,
Directed by Roger Corman and
(uncredited) Francis Ford Coppola,
Jack Hill and Monte Hellman

X—The Man With X-Ray Eyes
American International
Screenplay by Robert Dillion and
Ray Russell, *Produced and Directed*
by Roger Corman

1982

Vice Squad Avco Embassy
Screenplay by Sandy Howard,
Robert Vincent O'Neil and
Kenneth Peters
Produced by Brian Frankish
Directed by Gary A. Sherman

1983

Heart Like a Wheel
20th-Century Fox
Written, Produced and Directed by
Jonathan Kaplan

(As Writer)

Invasion of the Star Creatures
American International
Screenplay by Jonathan Haze
Produced by Berj Hagopian
Directed by Bruno Ve Sota

JACKIE JOSEPH
as Audrey Fulquard

BELLE JOSEPH WAS ONLY NINETEEN when her daughter Jackie was born. It was during the Depression, when times were hard for a lot of folks, but it seemed to Belle that she had more than her share: a nineteen-year-old, orphaned widow with child.

"She would have been a great grandmother," Jackie remarked. "Outrageous. She would have driven me nuts. But it would have been good."

Belle died of an operable cancer because the last time she saw a doctor was when Jackie was born and that hurt so she never saw one again.

During Jackie's teenage years she worked at night in her mother's liquor store on Seventh and San Pedro in downtown Los Angeles.

"That's why *Little Shop* seemed like such a natural for me," said Jackie. "I'd already done skid row."

It was during this time that Jackie developed an interest in acting. At nineteen she joined a little theater group, her tuition paid for by Belle with inventory from the store.

"My mother and I were arrested once. They were cracking down and a couple of new policemen thought we were lesbians, which was something you weren't supposed to be at the time," said Jackie. "They ended up taking us to dinner at the local dive."

Belle decided to get out of the liquor store business after a car careened into her window. The picture in the paper was nice, but enough was enough.

Meanwhile, Jackie went to school and joined a young actors group. During summer stock she met Joyce Jameson who was married to Billy Barns. Jackie became a part of Billy's review.

"I think Roger must have seen me in the Billy Barns review. Like *The Little Shop,* it has become a bit of memorabilia," said Jackie.

Q: And what was the Billy Barns review?

JOSEPH: Billy Barns was an incredible writer of music and lyrics. He wrote this satirical material. Now he's referred to as L.A.'s Stephen Sondheim. He was a UCLA kid. Slowly he gathered a nucleus of

Seymour thinks Audrey (Jackie Joseph) is a good kisser.

people who were all kids to do reviews. It was very popular. We even got paid, fifty dollars a week. People would come and come and come. It was a little naughty—not a lot. Now it's nothing. They made fun of personalities. And had a lot of really good songs we later found out 'cause they've held up over the years. Being a Billy Barns person now is almost like a badge of honor here in Los Angeles. I was sort of the ingenue. I was in my very early twenties. I had done "The Drunkard" and "The Wayward Way."

Q: Those ran for ...

JOSEPH: For thirty-six years, yes, I know. Well, I was only in for three of them, not all thirty-six. There must have been several sketches there where I was an innocent and that's what Roger wanted for *The Little Shop.* At least that's what I heard at this science fiction convention. They gave Roger an award and they invited the cast and we were all given things that would fit in our buttonholes, if we had a buttonhole. You know, Roger is such a nice gentleman. There's something elegant about him. I mean for all the wonderful, semi-trash that he grew up on and so cleverly made a living on, and the wonderful actors and directors and creative people and writers who grew through him ... he has an air of nobility about him. He looks like a high society person. And he talks like one. Maybe he *is* one. I don't even know. I think I was probably happier to see him than he was to see me.

Q: Why do you say that?

JOSEPH: I don't know. It might just be my personal problem or else ... I don't know if he socializes with any of his people. I know I never worked for him again. I don't think it was because I ever offended him. I think I just fit this particular niche. I would imagine a lot of his other films had either the basic sexy ladies or someone who's gonna turn into a wasp, may she rest in peace. I don't think he did too many comedies. But I did see *Bucket of Blood.* I was on the road in Edinburgh, Scotland. And I remembered a friend of mine was in *Bucket of Blood,* Tony Carbone, so I went to see it. I went to city college with him. We did "Country Girl" together.

Q: Were you the lead?

JOSEPH: Yes. Can you imagine what a reach that was? We got awards and everything. Tony was the director. The drunk was James Coburn. We had a real good group at LACC. Tony is a mysterious loss to the acting community because he had a wonderful quality. He did a couple of things for Roger with a lot of variety. I don't know what the problem was, if it was just the fates or what?

Q: What happened to him?

JOSEPH: I don't know. The last time I saw him (and this was quite a few years ago) he was a waiter in a health food restaurant. It made me feel awkward because I felt he was a star and I should be waiting on him. You know, you always remember people the way you first knew them. When I was in school Tony Carbone was the star of the first play I saw. Maybe he still acts.

I keep getting away from *Little Shop.*

Q: That's okay.

JOSEPH: Let's see, I was in New York. We had just finished playing a show which ran six months, and I got a call to do this movie. There would be two days and it was a detective movie.

Q: They said it was a detective movie?

JOSEPH: Yeah. Well, it was.

Q: I guess.

JOSEPH: The thing is, while I was flying from New York to L.A. they wrote a whole new movie. I never saw a script. They said: "You want to be in a movie?" And I said: "Oh, goody, goody." I'd only been in a few movies.

Q: What had you done?

JOSEPH: Let me think. I'd done a movie called *Suicide Battalion* with Touch Connors.

Q: I didn't know you were in that.

JOSEPH: Yes, I ... How do you know that? You've *heard* of *Suicide Battalion*?

Q: Of course.

JOSEPH: Well, I was Cho Cho, the Polynesian jungle girl that John Ashley married. I had a sarong and long hair and patent leather high heels, running through the jungle during the war. I think I worked longer on *Suicide Battalion* than I did *Little Shop* because no one could figure out how to write Polynesian. It was a funny job. I also did something called *Why Must I Die?*.

Q: Terry Moore and Debra Paget.

JOSEPH: Yes! You're good. Speaking of miscasting, I played a cigarette girl. I just loved it 'cause you get to wear the net hose and the little dinky outfit. I lied on the witness stand and because of my lying – I don't know why I hated Terry Moore but I told a fib on her and because of me – she went to the chair. I wasn't really remembered for that, though. Not that when *Little Shop* came out I suddenly had a career. They were both jobs. My first *real* movie, besides a Bible movie I did ...

Q: Wait. Let me hear.

JOSEPH: The Bible movie?

Q: Yes.

JOSEPH: I don't know what it was called but it was a Bible movie and it was actually going to pay. I remember I knew a month ahead of time. They sent me the script and I was the Egyptian mother of Moses who finds him in the bullrushes. But all I kept thinking was: I'm going to be in a movie. It was supposed to be one to three days and I thought maybe it would stretch to two. I had this eight o'clock call and I was home by noon. I arrived at the studio, they Egyptianed me up and took me on this set. The bullrushes were set in Coke cases. And there was a doll stuck in a basket. And it was something I had really built up. Never saw it, of course. But at least I'd been in the movies and I got my SAG card and I also got this job as a polar bear called Kewtee Bear from it. I had been the Easter Bunny at Robinson's for three years, a job that took me from L.A. to thirty-six cities including New York. When you're a theater arts major, you think New York City. You'd go *any* way. It was the first job I was ever kind of pushy about. I went to the audition with all these dwarves and Alan Reed. Alan Reed was the voice of Fred Flintstone. He was a very important actor on the radio. He was on *Allen's Alley*. Did a lot of films. Somehow he was involved in the McCarthy business.

Audrey thinks Seymour's plant is terrific, but Gravis Mushnik knows something that she doesn't.

talk about it. I just cared that I would be going on an airplane for the first time. I think Alan decided it would be much more fun to go with this dishy twenty-year-old girl than a midget, you know. It was nothing personal. But it hadn't dawned on him until I was fitted for the Kewtee Bear costume. I got my SAG card. Then, of

I think he was blacklisted for a while. He never really talked about it and I was just nineteen so I didn't know to

course, you think that people are going to call you and you're going to be in movies. Oh, I remember the first movie I ever did. It was a thing called *Speed Crazy*.

Q: Brett Halsey and Yvonne Lime.

JOSEPH: Yes! Yes. So good. Yvonne Lime Fedderson. She married Don Fedderson who produced "My Three Sons" and things like that. She's now very active in Child Help USA. I see her now at charity does when they need people to help. I was a truck stop girl that Brett Hasley meant a lot to. I remember having to stand, pretending to cheer at a race. I also remember the first scene I did was a master shot. You could be in college forever, which you usually are, and at that time no one told you what a mark was, what overlapping was... You didn't know what a master shot was, over-the-shoulder or close-ups. Well, we did the master and I went home. I didn't know they took away a piece of wall and turned everything around. You just guessed when they said *mark* and not to *overlap*. You don't want to ask because they'll think you're dumb. That was the type of work I did. There was a place called The Players' Ring Theater.

Q: On Santa Monica.

JOSEPH: Yes. So when I was fifteen and sixteen I would be doing plays there at night. It's interesting. All the time along, and you don't even know it, you're meeting people that affect you all through your life. I was working with Marvin Kaplan as his young girlfriend in "Once in a Lifetime." And Beverly Garland was the young leading lady.

Q: I wonder if Roger might have seen you there. He used to go to The Players' Ring.

JOSEPH: I don't think he really zeroed in on me there 'cause I didn't do really important stuff there. Just for a while, one play. I sang Welsh songs in a choir for "Corn is Green." Then I got there early the next morning to clean the bathrooms. You'd do anything ... anything to be part of the theater. I'm sure Roger saw me in the Billy Barns Review 'cause *that* was important. There were four men and four women. There was a sexy blonde (that was Joyce Jameson), a tall, raunchy redhead (Patti Regan), a dippy, little humorous person (Ann Gilbert) and the ingenue, who was me. We all got to wear low-cut black dresses. We thought it was low-cut at the time. Very individual personalities really showed. When I think of the work I have done, so much of it has always been someone who has been on the dim side. Sort of a gnat-brained, well-meaning person. After going to New York and doing the Billy Barns Show I got the call from Roger. I didn't even realize it was such a big part until I got there. Then when I heard they were going to shoot it in two days, Jackie Haze and I got together, for a couple of days, and memorized the script. We had to know it by heart. It was the first time I ever worked with three cameras. I think there were three cameras.

Q: It was like doing a play.

JOSEPH: It was. It was. There are only certain things I remember because it was just a job and I wanted to do my job. My basic instincts were, because I was not a method, dramatic actress, to do it as real as possible

and not to *try* to be funny. I didn't have the luxury of time that they had for the musical. And at that age I don't know that I would have had the wisdom to flesh it out. I remember we brought our own clothes. At the time there was this big, wonderful place called Jax. I remember dressing in these Jax clothes: tight-fitting and low-cut. Never in a million years did I suspect that I might look like a hooker. I just thought it was pretty, but I think there were some people around town who probably thought I was trying to get work any way possible. It's interesting no one has... Well, not recently, you wouldn't expect it, but in my youthful years, when I went on interviews and wore these Jax dresses with the tiny little straps, no one ever suggested, or if they did I didn't understand it, that I could get a job *if* ... There was no casting couch stuff. Every once in a while I think: Is that sad? I mean, I feel affronted that they never asked so I could say: "How dare you?" How dare they not ask. But back to Mr. Mushnik. We just sort of rehearsed. I think Roger was pre-lighting everything. I don't think we had a dressing room. To save time I had the next outfit hanging in a carpenter's booth on the sound stage so that I could quickly change and run in to the next set. There's only one

Copyright © 1960 The Filmgroup, Inc.

Seymour, Mushnik and Audrey (Jackie Joseph) admire Seymour's creation, Audrey Junior – a cross between a buttercup and a Venus's Flytrap.

moment I remember being depressed. When you're young and in the business you really trust the different artists, like the make-up artist. I think his name was Harry Wolfe, or something. He was doing this make-up and I noticed I was getting these wider and wider eyebrows. I was starting to sweat because it was a big part and I knew it was a silly movie, but I was starting to be a little nervous. But I kept thinking he must know what he's doing because he does it and I don't do it very often, and so I didn't say anything. I beat around the bush a little and finally asked him if he'd done a lot of movies. He said, "Oh, yes. Tons and tons." He'd worked for Roger a lot. I asked him what women he'd made up and he said, "Oh, you're the first one. Usually I make monsters."

Q: Maybe he was trying to turn you into a werewolf.

JOSEPH: He was doing the best he could. I snuck into the ladies' room and diminished the humongous black eyebrows. You never want to touch the work. I didn't. I was very timid. And I'm still not real brazen or anything. I learned to bring my own make-up thing in case I got stuck with someone who doesn't believe in eye-liner or something, since I disappear without it. One of the little girls – you know, those flower girls – Tammy became a casting director. I think she even helped me get a cereal commercial or something like that. Mrs. Fishtwanger, or whatever, was married (or *is* married) to a prominent producer. Shame on me for not having the name on the tip of my tongue.

Q: Was there much flubbing?

JOSEPH: No. It was a very natural role. It was real easy. Maybe I should credit Chuck Griffith a little. I didn't know him at all. I didn't know anybody. It may have been written so that it was so easy to be natural. Maybe it was a good combination. It was very easy for me to work with the script. I didn't find myself saying: "I want to change this line." I just did it and didn't question the ridiculous parts. I figured that was her honesty. I guess that's what makes people shake their heads and say: "That dumb movie." Everybody went with the ridiculous.

Q: Did you see the play?

JOSEPH: I was there at the opening night of the Westwood version. Jackie Haze and I were treated royally. It's funny. A lot of the P.R. people had never heard of the movie.

Q: Peculiar.

JOSEPH: I thought so. I was waiting for them to call 'cause I thought they would want us there. It didn't make sense for them *not* to want us there. Finally, I called the P.R. lady and said, "Hi, I'm Jackie Joseph." She said, "Where are you from?" I said, "Burbank. I was in the original movie and I was wondering if you were going to have the cast at the opening in Westwood." She said, "Well, I really don't know. No one has said anything about it." I realized it had been a presumption on my part. Then I was talking to a friend of mine who is a writer and critic for the *Times* and happened to have mentioned, laugh-ingly, what a silly thing I'd done and she was outraged. Her name is Carolyn Cee. Carolyn called the *L.A. Reader* and asked if they would like a story on *The Little Shop of Horrors* opening in Westwood, along with the stars of the movie? Then she called the P.R. people to tell them she was doing the piece for the *Reader* and that she wanted to bring the stars of the movie and the same woman that I had talked to said: "Oh, isn't that funny. Some woman from Burbank called and said *she* was the star of the movie." Like I was some fraud. Anyway, the woman from Burbank *did* get to go and was treated augustly by the writers and the people in the cast and everyone.

Q: One of my favorite scenes in the original movie is where you and Mel Welles are in that restaurant.

JOSEPH: The dialogue there is really strange. And I was just so glad to have something to eat. There was a big rush to finish before New Year's Eve because starting in 1960 you'd have to pay residuals. It was just on the edge of midnight 1959 when we finished. It was a major rush to beat residuals. I didn't know that until it started playing on TV a lot and I asked if I got paid anything and they said no. I enjoyed working with Dick Miller. Dick is a terribly funny, easy-going guy. He's had a wonderful career. I think he should be a major star. We recently worked together in two films as husband and wife. We did *Gremlins*. He was Mr. Fudderman, the snow-plow operator and I was Mrs. Fudderman. We were both dashed into by a snow-plow which was funny. We also did a movie called *Get Crazy* which Alan Arkush did. It was a weird rock movie but interesting. And we played this nice couple. Both of these young directors, Joe Dante and Alan Arkush, and even, perhaps, Mike Fennel who was the on-line producer of *Gremlins*, are *Little Shop* fans. I could just see them all sitting around their little rooms saying, "Guess what funny people we used in our movie?" I was pleased, of course. It's harder when you're older. There's just not that many roles, especially when you've niched yourself. Whenever I do get a role that's just a normal woman instead of someone just off-center, I'm pleased to do it because I need the insurance.

Q: Recently you've become active in helping battered women and before that it was Active Mothers for Animals. How did this all come about?

JOSEPH: I was doing the "Doris Day Show" which was a lark because it was right after I declared that I was not going to work anymore.

Q: Why was that?

JOSEPH: Something in my non-communicative head thought that maybe something wasn't good in my marriage and if I didn't work any-more it might be better.

Q: You were married to Ken Berry.

JOSEPH: That's right. So I just stopped working. When we got mar-ried and we had children I decided that I wouldn't go on the road, I wouldn't work in theater, and I wouldn't do a series.

Q: How many children did you have?

JOSEPH: We adopted two children. Now they're 23 and 24. John Kenneth and Jennifer Kate. Jennifer Kate is married to Bill Bateman who's known as Buster of a rock group called The Blasters. So I get to introduce him as my son-in-law, Buster of the Blasters. He's very kind. Better a kindly blaster than a surly lawyer, you know. Very

Mushnik wants to fire Seymour, but Audrey (Jackie Joseph) thinks he should give Seymour a chance to "resurrect" himself.

sweet, gentle fellow. "Blaster" as in it's a blast, as opposed to blowing up the world. I was pleased to hear that. Anyway, I had quit working and when "Mayberry R.F.D." was cancelled, Ken was so bereft. And rightly so. It was a very highly rated show and CBS just decided to sweep all the country shows away. It had been the first time he had felt home free. He said to me, "I think you'd better think about going back to work." And it's as if God said, "Okay," 'cause the phone rang and my agent was saying "I know you don't want to do a series but this one starts to shoot at twelve." It was without an interview or anything. They just asked if I'd be a regular on "The Doris Day Show." That was the last two years of her series. At the time I was in the Parents' Association of the Oakwood Lower School. In fact, I quit my job at ABC. I used to show their movies every morning.

Q: I remember. One morning you ran *On Borrowed Time* and when you came back on at the end of it you were in tears.

JOSEPH: Yes. The show was called "The Prize Movie." When both my kids were ready for school I needed to drive them to school and I needed to go to the parents' meetings. I didn't realize that all the parents didn't go. I mean, there was like only a handful. But I still wanted to go and be this participating kind of parent. It was not a real early parenthood. We were thirty when we got John. We wanted to do it right. Not that it turned out that way. In John's class was Gina Basehart, daughter of Richard and Diana Basehart. They were very involved with humane activities. And something terrible happened at the L.A. shelters. So between the Baseharts and Doris I got involved. We decided to form a group that had actors involved so that, perhaps, our activities would make the TV news. And when all the actors went to City Hall for hearings it made the front page. There were major changes. Wonderful changes in the city and county shelters. It could always be better but because of our organization they don't have the decompression

chambers anymore. Those were evil, icky things. And now they're something of the past. So we continue on. I'm still in touch with Doris. She's having such a wonderful life in Carmel. She calls me "Jocko." She has one house for herself and one for her animals. And a lot of her old staff have found their way up there. She was very good to work with. And although other people have moved on, especially Richard Basehart — excuse me, I have a terrible sense of humor. He made great souffles and he loved animals and he was a wonderful actor.

Q: How did you get involved with displaced women?

JOSEPH: Displaced Homemakers is the Federal term as far as funding goes. Even though it sounds like refugees from Albania, it's really half the women in America plus. The way I got into that is that my ex-husband was on the road with Patti McLeod who is married to Gavin McLeod. Gavin called and said he wanted a divorce. She was so shocked and bereft and bereft and bereft and bereft that Ken couldn't understand why, at some point, she wouldn't just say onward and upward. Some of us don't show it as much. You pretend you're okay and hide your feelings. I was not conspicuously bereft when Ken and I later broke up. Ken had Patti call me to show her that you didn't have to weep all the time. For about a year we were phone friends. She called one day and said there was another lady who was married to an actor who thought it would be interesting to get a bunch of women together who were married to celebrities and share feelings. Because no one else seems to understand the publicness of it all. I realized much later there were a lot of things I still hadn't tended to in terms of self and stuff like that. Like just the most important stuff. Because of that first meeting there was a lot of energy generated, and a lot of caring, and a lot of feeling. We realized that it would be good to meet more often. Then we got a name because it seemed necessary. People were calling us names so we thought we'd get one of our own. It's still a misunderstood gathering. There are still people who think we get together to see how we can *get* our ex-husbands. What it really is ...

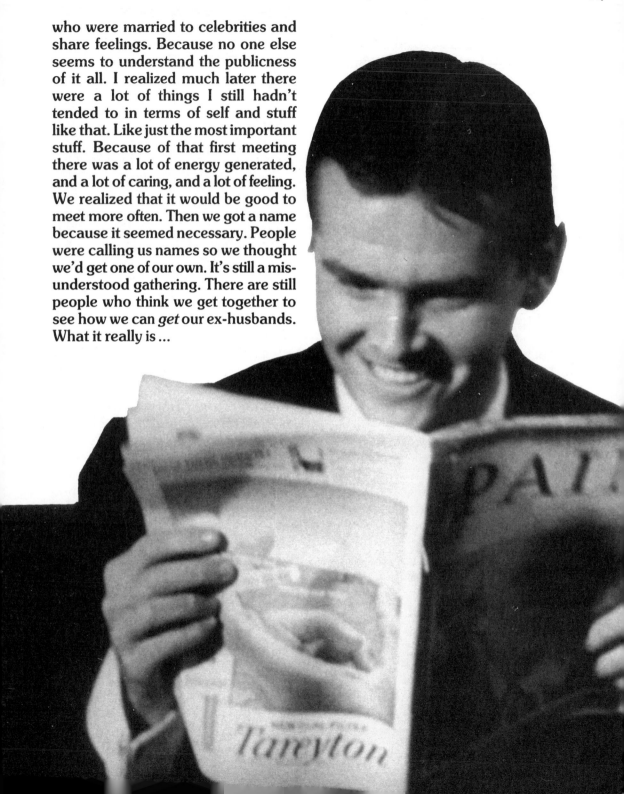

Q: Is to *forget.*

JOSEPH: Yeah. It's to show you how to let things go. And for your own sake go through your anger and then let it go. We don't seek out people. They seem to find us. And there's always some women who think they don't need help until it happens to them because no one thinks it's going to happen. It's not in anybody's master plan. It's one of those things people have to go through and societally feel they must feel guilty and bad and failed. And whatever pain they're going through is just the breaks. The truth of it is it's a physical condition, like an illness. It's legitimate to feel crazy for a while and to feel your whole soul has been sucked out, because it *has* been. Just hearing it said out loud validates those feelings and then people can go ahead and be better. It's important to know you're not the only one. People are just dying and becoming street people, and addicts.

A very sad lot for women who are scared out of their brains because they're older and they've never worked and never been on their own. There are dumped animals and there are dumped women. They both need new beginnings. We've slowly, always by request, been going to conferences for the displaced home-makers network in Washington. Now we're working with the state of California through the vocational education department. It's a very quirky thing. It's like a mission: to link needy people to the services that are available.

Q: How long have you been doing that now?

JOSEPH: Almost five years. Isn't that funny. It certainly wasn't planned, you know. Now we have to get child care and we have to get industry...

Courtesy Mark Thomas McGee Collection

It looks like Nicholson is preparing for his role in The Shining.

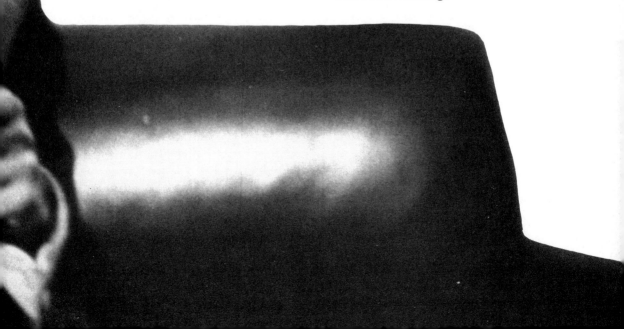

Jackie Joseph reunites with Dick Miller in Gremlins.

You know, we can train all these wonderful older women and they're ready to conquer the world but people still want that front office chick. The whole office has to take a big swerve. Which it is. You have to be patient because things just happen when they will but sometimes you have to shove them along a little.

A week after this conversation, a tribute to Jackie Joseph was held at the Variety Arts Center. There was a lunch and a "secret something" from Billy Barns. In attendance: Betty White, Earl Holliman, Sybil Brand, Stephanie Edwards, Carolyn Cee, Dick and Patti Van Patten and, of course, members of L.A.D.I.E.S. Jackie felt a little funny about being honored for the work she'd done. But it didn't seem at all out of line that someone, or a lot of someones decided to say thanks. She's earned it.

Produced by Hal B. Wallis
Directed by Michael Curtiz

1959

Speed Crazy Allied Artists
Screenplay by Richard Bernstein
and George Waters
Produced by Richard Bernstein
Directed by William Hole, Jr.

1960

Why Must I Die?
American International
Screenplay by George W. Waters
and Richard Bernstein
Produced by Richard Bernstein
Directed by Roy Del Ruth

1967

A Guide for the Married Man
20th-Century Fox
Screenplay by Frank Tarloff
Produced by Frank McCarthy
Directed by Gene Kelly

Who's Minding the Mint?
Columbia
Screenplay by R. S. Allen and
Harvey Bullock
Produced by Norman Maurer
Directed by Howard Morris

1968

With Six You Get an Eggroll
National General
Screenplay by Gwin Bagni
Produced by Martin Melcher
Directed by Howard Morris

The Split Metro-Goldwyn-Mayer
Screenplay by Robert Sabaroff
Produced by Irwin Winkler and
Robert Chartoff
Directed by Gordon Flemyng

FILMOGRAPHY

1958

Suicide Battalion
American International
Written and Produced by Lou Rusoff
Directed by Edward L. Cahn

King Creole Paramount
Screenplay by Herbert Baker and
Michael Vincente Gazzo
from Harold Robbins' novel
"A Stone For Danny Fisher"

1970

The Cheyenne Social Club
National General
Screenplay by James Lee Barrett
Produced and Directed by Gene Kelly

1983

Get Crazy Avco Embassy
Screenplay by Danny Opatoshu,
Henry Rosenbaum and David Taylor
Produced by Hunt Lowry
Directed by Allan Arkush

1984

Gremlins Warner Brothers
Screenplay by Christopher Columbus
Produced by Michael Finnell
Directed by Joe Dante

MEL WELLES
as Gravis Mushnik

POSSIBLY THE FUNNIEST OF THE original *Little Shop* characters is the perplexed and verbose skid row flower emporium owner, portrayed by New York-born Mel Welles. His larger-than-life portrait of a hard-luck merchant who dreams of owning a flower "saloon" in Beverly Hills is a standout.

Welles was a graduate of the University of West Virginia. He had a PhD in psychology but after a year of practice he decided the profession was "full of it." He began looking for something else to do with his life. Something in "The Arts" seemed like a good idea but he'd been told often enough that he had a tin ear, so singing was out, and painting pictures that didn't sell had no appeal to him, so when someone suggested he try acting, he figured it was the best of his options. "I have a photographic memory so learning dialogue is no problem," Welles said.

Always a character actor, Welles appeared in *Appointment in Honduras* (1953), *Abbott and Costello Meet the Mummy* (1955), and *Designing Woman* (1957) before hooking up with Roger Corman.

"The great thing about Roger was that he was always good for a few week's work when you were between jobs," Welles remarked. "You didn't make a lot of money working for him but things cost a lot less back then. And in those days Roger always had a picture going. He was American International's only supplier when they started, so he made ten, twelve pictures a year for them. The deal was that upon delivery of the picture he would get fifty thousand dollars negative pick-up plus a fifteen thousand advance on the foreign sales. So he made every picture for under sixty-five thousand. In fact, every third picture he would send out and get it bootlegged for twenty-eight thousand or thirty thousand, then deliver it and get the sixty-five thousand. Not that he didn't share in further profits but Sam Arkoff was

As Sir Bop, Mel Welles rattles off hep talk a mile a minute. From Rock All Night.

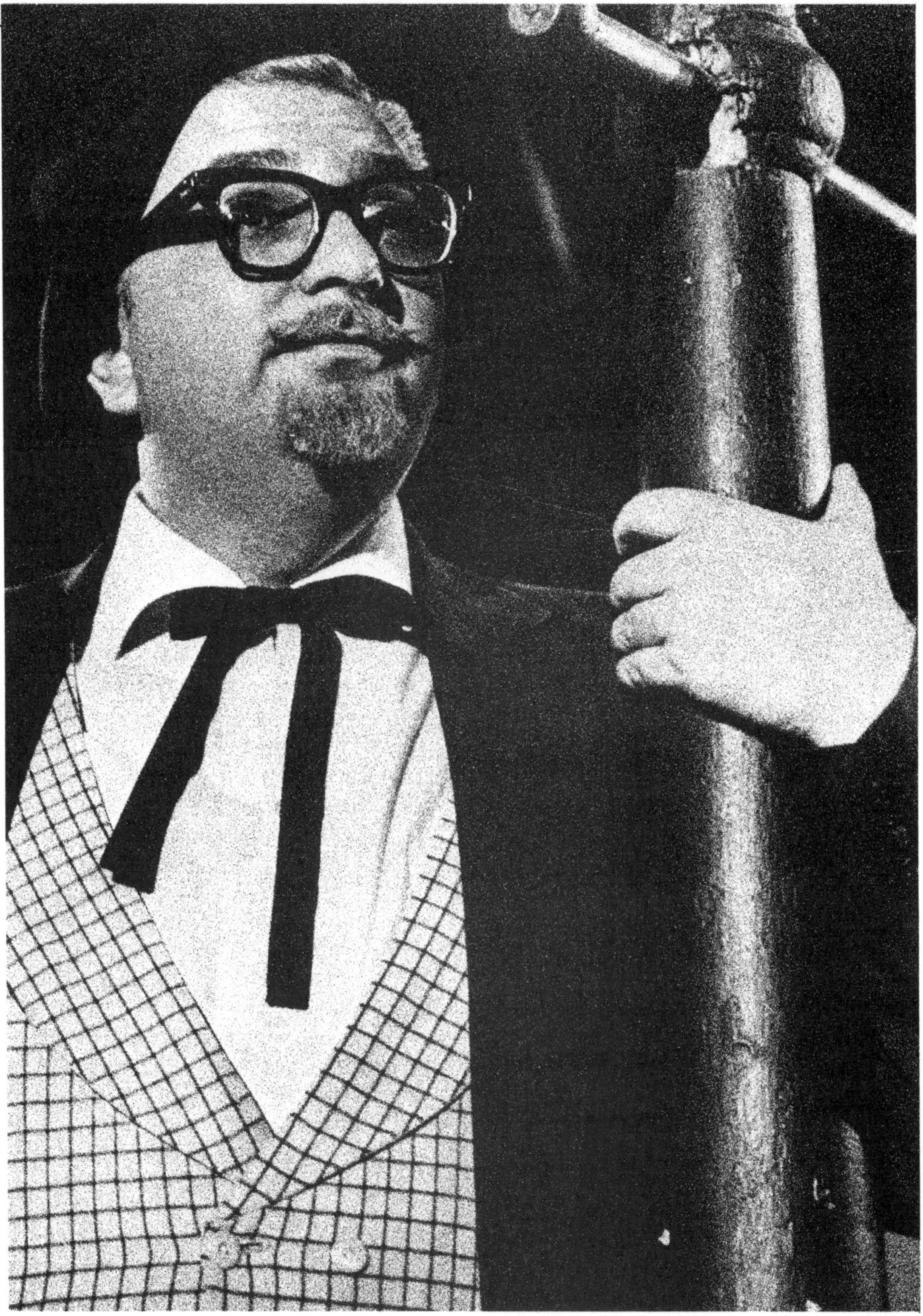

a pretty clever guy too, so you really never saw much later other than what you got up front.

Q: Tell me about your first Corman film, *The Attack of the Crab Monsters.*

WELLES: To me the picture was a piece of fluff. It was fun. It was like a comic book. Most of the people in it had fun. I think it was Ed Nelson's first picture out here. He was an announcer in New Orleans who'd done a couple of pictures for the Woolner Brothers and Roger when they went on location. He decided to try his hand at Hollywood. He came up to Roger's office and we were doing *Attack of the Crab Monsters* and BANGO! I think he was one of the sailors in it.

Q: And the crab.

WELLES: What are you talking about?

Q: Ed Nelson played the crab.

WELLES: Who told you that?

Q: I don't really remember. I may have read it.

WELLES: You film fans come up with these things. I don't know where they come from.

Q: I've heard it from a number of different people, I'm sure. Specifically, I asked Beach Dickerson about it and he claimed he and Nelson took turns playing the crab.

WELLES: Maybe it's true then, I don't know. I was there and I don't remember that. The crab was on wires.

Q: But somebody had to be beneath it.

WELLES: Why, if it was on wires?

Q: Because something had to propel it. The wires were to make the pincher wiggle and lift the eyelids. There's a scene in the picture where, between two rocks, you can see a pair of legs.

WELLES: I remember they couldn't get the crab to sink. They took it to Marineland and tried to push it underwater and the arms broke off. I think Roger paid four hundred dollars to have it made.

Q: Do your remember anything else about the picture?

WELLES: From my standpoint it was the least colorful Roger Corman picture in terms of behind the cameras, because it went basically the smoothest. I don't remember Roger screaming much. Roger was like a skipper on a yacht where you really don't have time to baby people. On a yacht you might yell at your friend in an ugly manner, you might shout or bark so that the thing is done *now*, 'cause it needs to be done *now*. So Roger, realizing that he had five or six days to shoot a film, and limited money, was like that skipper on a yacht. So when things are not going at the right pace he would yell, not out of anger, but because whatever it was, it had to be done immediately. It's important that you include that because a lot of people read him wrong. I found that to be one of his most admirable qualities – that he was able to keep that yacht moving. Part of the Corman myth is that he was a lucky man. With the Midas touch and all of that. The truth is that Roger Corman was a totally effective filmmaker in terms of the business end of it, not in terms of the quality factor because this conversation is not about that. As a producer and later as a director, he executed his job of solving problems within the

because he could make an emergency decision no matter what. If things were going wrong and he might lose a half day production, his ability to make a decision that would get the

parameters of his authority with the greatest amount of efficiency. He wasn't really a very good director of actors because I don't think he ever really understood actors, although he did go out of his way to take a course from Jeff Corey so he wasn't totally insensitive to the problem. But as a camera director he was phenomenal, first and foremost

Leola Wendorff (Mrs. Shiva) and Mel from
The Little Shop of Horrors.

picture done was remarkable. Even if he had to rip out twenty or thirty pages of the script. Even if there had to be an on-the-spot change in the entire concept of the project. This is the part that everybody misses about Roger. He had a good time solving

problems. Which allowed him to be blunt, abrupt, brusque, sometimes brutal in the decision that he made. But it permitted him to do that because he was doing his job and he was doing it effectively.

Q: Your next picture for Corman was *The Undead*, which was certainly one of the most unusual pictures he ever made.

WELLES: If you're going to understand that picture you have to go back to the events that were going on in the world at the time. That picture was based on the Bridey Murphy phenomenon. There was a woman (I don't remember her name) who was hypnotised and under hypnosis described her previous life as a person named Bridey Murphy. So Chuck Griffith wrote this marvelous script and all of the dialogue was written in verse. It made that medieval regression part come off very ethereal, very Hansel and Gretal-ish, and would have been very charming. Roger lost his nerve. Didn't want to do it. I rememer all of us were very disappointed. Bruno Ve Sota especially. Also, casting Pamela Duncan and Richard Garland in the roles wasn't really terrific either.

Q: What about *Rock All Night*?

WELLES: My part was originally written for Dick Buckley. Dick Buckley was a guy I used to write for. He was an outrageous comedian that talked in hip talk and yet looked like an English Lord. But, as usual, Dick was

Here, Mel plays an addle-brained gravedigger comforting Pamela Duncan in The Undead.

kind of flakey about his movements and he disappeared. So I decided to play the part myself. Nobody else could. In those days nobody else understood hip talk. The only people that ever used any kind of hip words on television were Frank Sinatra and Steve Allen and they used words like "dig." And that was it. So we're right in the middle of the beat generation and beatniks were the only ones who understood the language and Roger got very scared that nobody would understand the picture. So I wrote the first dictionary of hip talk – The Hiptionary. There were five million of those sent out with the picture as a move for everybody to be able to understand not only what I said, but there was a lot of hip talk in the picture. If I'd have done that for a major studio, I would get the royalty off that. I didn't even get ten dollars for it. And I was, at the time, really the nation's authority on hip talk.

Q: Did you know there was a scene from that film used in a movie called *Let the Good Times Roll*?

WELLES: No.

Q: It's a shot of you rattling off a lot of hip talk. It's pretty funny. Didn't you also write some hip dialogue for *High School Confidential*?

WELLES: Yes. There's a long bit with John Drew Barrymore giving a history lesson in the classroom. I wrote all of that. I was also the technical advisor on that picture. I showed the actors how to roll a joint and explained the effects of marijuana, but the producer wasn't much interested in being accurate.

Q: I understand *Rock All Night* was originally a television show.

WELLES: That's right. It was something that Roger bought. There's a guy named Bert Nelson in the picture. He was a bouncer at The Interlude nightclub and I got him a job in the picture. Later, Bert went to Europe because he was into muscle building and he wanted to play in those gladiator pictures, those Steve Reeves-type things. Today, he lives in Germany, and he's a multi-millionaire. He opened up an Italian restaurant in Berlin and now he owns a chain of Italian restaurants in Europe. And half of an Italian frozen pizza business. And he's a Jewish kid from the south.

Q: Which brings us to *The Little Shop of Horrors.*

WELLES: The interesting side-line on *Little Shop of Horrors* is that after the picture was made, Roger wagged his finger at us for a long time with an I-told-you-so attitude because he had difficulty getting the film distributed. The exhibitors thought it was anti-Semitic. They thought it was anti-Semitic for two reasons. One, we had a character in it called Mrs. Shiva who had relatives that were always dying. In the Jewish faith, when somebody dies and you mourn them, it's called sitting shivah. And her name was Mrs. S. Shiva which was a *Mad* magazine play on it. That was one thing they thought was pretty irreverent. The second thing was I was playing a Jewish character and by the time I discovered that the plant was eating people, the place was full and the cash register was going and I

decided not to call the police because of the money I was making. Exhibitors took that to be an anti-Semitic thing. The way the picture eventually got released was when American International bought Mario Bava's first horror picture, *Black Sunday*. It was an awful picture but it had the best campaign that I had ever seen up to that date on a low budget exploitation motion picture. They mounted a beautiful campaign. But they needed another picture because in those days you released everything in double features. So they agreed to take *Little Shop of Horrors*. But what happened was that people began to talk about *Little Shop of Horrors* and they began to come just to see *Little Shop of Horrors* and not even stay for *Black Sunday*. It became a kind of cult film. It played for weeks at campuses because it caught the imagination of the young people, the hipsters of the time. It's amazing to me when I go to see the picture today with a group of people younger than the picture who understand some of the gags that were, at the time, topical. Like the gag about the Japanese cranberry farmer. You know, Jonathan says he got the seeds that turn into the plant from a Japanese cranberry farmer. I'm sure it's not understood. It gets a laugh but not for the right reason. The right reason is that, at that time, there was a cancer scare over a carcinogen from some insecticide or pesticide they'd used on the cranberry farms in Georgia. It was supposed to have this cancer-producing effect so people, like for a whole year, didn't buy cranberries. Thanksgiving dinner was without cranberry sauce. Everybody was scared. So that's why it was funny then. Now it's just a funny idea; a Japanese cranberry farmer. But at the time it got a big laugh because of what had just happened.

Q: Chuck Griffith said that you and Dick Miller ad-libbed a lot of your dialogue.

WELLES: That's not true.

Q: Why would he say it?

WELLES: He doesn't remember. He wrote every word. The brilliant thing that Chuck did was that he wrote that part *for* me. We were best friends. And when I used to do my Jewish accent around him I used to have certain expressions. And he knew them all because they broke him up all the time. He incorporated them into the script. I didn't have to make up one word. I may have ad-libbed a line or two but I memorized the dialogue and I was so meticulous about rehearsing it that I was really good in the part to the point where the material really sounded like it was being processed by my brain, which is what an actor's supposed to do. You know, there's an edge of madness to this business. The edge of madness is that even a low budget picture, like Corman makes, today costs one million two hundred thousand dollars. For one million two hundred thousand dollars you could open five luxury restaurants. You could put the down payment on two office buildings. You could open a chain of men's clothing stores. You could open up a manufacturing plant. You could invest in land development. You could do a lot of things with a million two hundred thousand dollars. But instead you wind up with two small cans about eighteen inches by two feet by another two feet. And there are five reels of film in these two small cans that you can fit into a closet. And it could be worthless. Or it could be worth three hundred million dollars. So that causes a kind of edge of madness.

In addition to his work as an actor, Welles has directed a few films: *Code of Silence* (1958), *Island of the Doomed* (1966), and *Lady Frankenstein* (1971). He can still occasionally be seen in things like *Smokey Bites the Dust* (1981), *Dr. Heckyl and Mr. Hype* (1980), and *Chopping Mall* (1987) but he's more active in cartoons now, supplying voices for animated characters.

FILMOGRAPHY
(As Performer)

1953

Appointment in Honduras
RKO Radio Pictures
Screenplay by Karen De Wolfe
Produced by Benedict Bogeaus
Directed by Jacques Tourneur

1955

Abbott and Costello Meet the Mummy Universal-International
Screenplay by John Grant
Produced by Howard Cristie
Directed by Charles Lamont

The Silver Chalice
Warner Brothers
Screenplay by Lesser Samuels
based on Thomas Costain's novel
Produced and Directed by
Victor Saville

Soldier of Fortune
20th-Century Fox
Screenplay by Ernest K. Gann
from his novel
Produced by Buddy Adler
Directed by Edward Dmytryk

1957

Attack of the Crab Monsters
Allied Artists
Screenplay by Charles B. Griffith
Produced and Directed by
Roger Corman

The Undead American International
Screenplay by Charles B. Griffith
and Mark Hanna
Produced and Directed by
Roger Corman

1958

The Brothers Karamazov
Metro-Goldwyn-Mayer
Produced by Pandro S. Berman
Written (from the novel by
Dostoyevsky*) and Directed by*
Richard Brooks

1962

**Hemingway's Adventures of
a Young Man** 20th-Century Fox
Screenplay by A. E. Hotchner
Produced by Jerry Wald
Directed by Martin Ritt

*Mel comes face to face with a giant crab
and doesn't like it. From Roger Corman's
Attack of the Crab Monsters.*

1965

The She-Beast (a.k.a. **Revenge of
the Blood Beast**) Europix
Screenplay by Michael Byron
Produced by Paul Maslansky
Directed by Michael Reeves

1980

Dr. Heckyl and Mr. Hype Cannon
Written and Directed by
Charles B. Griffith
Produced by Menachem Golan
and Yoram Globus

1986

Chopping Mall (a.k.a. **Killbots**)
Concorde
Screenplay by Jim Wynorski
and Steve Mitchell
Produced by Julie Corman
Directed by Jim Wynorski

(As Director)

1960

Code of Silence Sterling
Screenplay by Norman Toback
and Allan Adrian
Produced by Berj Hagopian
Directed by Mel Welles

1966

Island of the Doomed
Allied Artists
Screenplay by Stephen Schmidt
Produced by George Ferrer
Directed by Mel Welles

1972

Lady Frankenstein New World
Screenplay by Edward di Lorenzo
Produced by Harry Cushing
Directed by Mel Welles

DICK MILLER
as Bourson Fouch

THERE ARE A FEW ACTORS WHO always bring a smile to the lips whenever people see them on the screen. Dick Miller is one of them. Throughout his career Dick has played a variety of roles, and performs well no matter what sort of character he's playing, but for these authors' money he's never been more enjoyable than when he's playing a fast-talking, street-wise salesman. His part in *The Terminator* may have been brief but it was memorable. "I got more action out of that two minute scene than just about anything else," Dick said. "Everybody in the country saw *Terminator*."

He was born in the Bronx on December 25, 1928, started singing when he was eight years old. Not professionally — just singing and dancing around the house. He knew then he wanted to be in show business but he went to school and studied other things. He had a degree in psychology and worked at that for a while. "I realized," Dick said, "that I couldn't handle all the crazy people. So I went into show business where there are no crazy people. Right?"

Dick was in the Navy during WWII. He was seventeen. When he got out he bummed around for a while and when the money started running out he figured he'd let Uncle Sam educate him. He looked in the newspaper and discovered upholsterers earned two and a half dollars an hour, which during those days was nothing to sneeze at. He went to the New York School of Upholstery, signed all the papers, then found out there were no night classes. Getting up at eight in the morning was out of the question. He didn't go to bed until two or three in the morning. Dick still had it in his mind that he was in show business. He was writing songs for Bobby Van and he was playing drums and singing in clubs. So Dick looked on his list of schools and saw, next to the New York School of Upholstery, the New York Theater School where he could get an eleven o'clock class. Jason Robards Jr. and Tom Poston were his instructors.

"I started working right after I got out of school," Dick said. He was writing, producing and directing on radio and television shows simultaneously. "It was a busy time. It was good." And he was earning a pretty good living. So he decided to try his luck in California. For a year and a half he didn't earn a nickel.

At that time Dick didn't think of himself as an actor. In his mind he was a writer. Forry Ackerman introduced him to a guy who was producing a science fiction anthology for TV. Dick didn't think much of TV. To him there was Broadway, which was real acting, and movies which was something he wanted to do.

The producer didn't want scripts,

Dick Miller as Mr. Fudderman in Joe Dante's Gremlins.

he wanted outlines so Dick hammered out ten outlines that he doled out once a week at a hundred dollars a pop.

Q: So how'd you finally break into the movies?

MILLER: Jonathan Haze, who had been a buddy of mine in New York, came out here a little before I did. We met out here and we were bumming around and he said he was working

Seymour rebels at Dr. Farb's sadistic methods.

Courtesy Mark Thomas McGee Collection

for this young producer-director, Roger Corman. He said "Come on up to the office." So I met Roger. It was laughs. We were sitting around and I thought he was a nice guy. It was a very social thing. He said, "What do you do?" And I said I was a writer. He said, "I don't need any scripts. I got scripts." "That's too bad," I said. "What do you need? I can run the camera and I can act." So my first picture was *Apache Woman*, which in itself is a great story. I played an Indian the first week. We

finished that crazy thing and Roger said, "You wanna play a cowboy?" And I said, "You doing another picture?" He said, "No. It's the same picture." So I came back as a cowboy. The way it was originally set up I would have gone out and shot myself.

Q: That would have been great.

MILLER: It would have been marvelous. We did a couple of westerns before we did any science fiction.

Q: The first one was *It Conquered the World* with the terrifying ice-cream cone monster.

MILLER: The carrot. Everybody's got another name for it.

Q: Paul Blaisdell called it Beulah. Chuck Griffith said he called it Denny Dimwit.

MILLER: He called everything Denny Dimwit. It was supposed to be larger. This was the top half of it. And they didn't know what to do with the body. It was just a head. Roger said, "If you put a body on this thing it'll be monstrous. What are we going to do with it? We can't shoot it. We can't have anybody work in the same scene with it." Maybe Blaisdell wanted six dollars more to make a body. I don't know. They put a fringe around the bottom of it and that was it. They just used the head. They had to move the arms up higher.

Q: It was unique.

MILLER: It was effective.

Q: Rock All Night was your first big part, wasn't it?

MILLER: It was my first starring role.

Q: You got good reviews.

MILLER: Got monstrous reviews. I couldn't believe it. If that picture was made today ... You know how many little pictures are made today with kids and they come out and the next thing you see these kids are starring in great movies. It's hard to understand the business. But really, these were B movies. People knew they were going to see a cheapie little film. That's what they were supposed to be; the bottom half of the bill. Nobody ever thought of sleepers. There were no sleepers. A picture could have been the greatest picture in the world and it wouldn't've happened. It was a different time, as different as the talkies from the silent movies. This was an era when they were making these little movies specifically for that purpose and nobody ever thought of anyone coming out of those pictures as being hot. This picture for some reason came out and I got marvelous reviews: "Only the performance of Dick Miller makes this a worthwhile evening." Things like that. It was unbelievable. I got myself a big agent out of it. I took out a full page ad in *Variety*. Arkoff and Nicholson approved the copy. Then later they read the ad and said, "What the hell did you write here: *Only* the performance of Dick Miller makes this picture worthwhile. We're not going to pay for that!" I said, "I'm not asking you to pay for it. I wanted you to pay half. Give me a break on this thing."

Q: How did that one come about?

MILLER: I'd been doing a bunch of pictures. The picture previous to that was *Thunder Over Hawaii*, which was really a good picture. I think the story and the acting and everything would hold up today.

Q: I must digress for just a bit. Why does everybody that worked on that picture call it by that title? It was first released as *Naked Paradise*.

MILLER: It was released as *Naked Paradise* and they didn't think that was a classy enough title after they viewed the picture and they decided to make it *Thunder Over Hawaii* as an action title. Roger does that today. He releases a picture in Georgia some place, pulls it back and changes the title. This was the first time *that* happened. I was ashamed of the title. I thought people would think I was making a ...

Dick Miller (center) in his first starring role in Rock All Night.

Q: Porno picture?

MILLER: Something. Yeah. You know. Actually, *Naked Paradise* is a great title. But Roger didn't think it had enough action to it. *Naked Paradise* kind of gave it a romantic quality. You know, tropical islands; some kind of idyllic love story. He wanted something with a little more action to it. Thunder over ANYTHING is an action title: over Arizona, over New York, over New Mexico. Everybody worked on a "Thunder Over" picture. It took me years. I always used to say *Naked Paradise*. Then I'd get the opposite response. "Oh, yes, it was released as *Naked Paradise* but ..." I knew that. It did turn out to be a good picture. And I got some good reviews on it. We had real sneak previews in those days. We'd go out in the toolies somewhere, some little theater in Newhall or someplace, and show it and get a reaction. Marketing, I guess, was Roger's forte. He knew what he was doing, so these little sneaks really meant something to him. If they didn't like something he'd cut out the scene if he could afford to cut it. If the whole picture wasn't sixty-eight minutes. I was standing in the lobby, and Beverly Garland (who I admire) said: "You really walked away with that one. You really came out looking great." I said, "Aw, you're kidding." And she said: "No. You're really good." And she said it loud enough and with enough enthusiasm that I think Roger picked up on it. A month or so later the picture was released and I guess I got a lot of good feedback.

Q: I also understand you had a decent place to stay for a change while you were making the picture.

MILLER: We were in the Cocoa Palms which, on Kauai, was *the* hotel. It was just beautiful. You didn't have single rooms in those days, you had to buddy up, so naturally Jonathan

and I were buddying up, trying to tear up the island with the little Hawaiian girls. It was nice. We did two pictures back to back there. *She-Gods of Shark Reef* was the other one.

Q: I didn't know you were in that.

MILLER: I wasn't. We went out early. Roger said, "You can come out and sit around for three weeks while we do one picture and then we'll do your picture." He said we wouldn't get paid but we'd get the accommodations. So it was a little vacation. And there were things we did on the other picture. Jonathan and I were both very athletic. We'd both boxed. We had similar backgrounds. When we came to Hollywood if they asked, "Can you ride?" you say "Yes." "Can you fall off a horse?" "Yeah." "Can you fall off a cliff?" "Yeah." We did it all. Mostly because we were young and strong. We never thought about getting hurt. I got hurt on pictures. I think back now – broken wrists, broken ankles, broken tailbone, busted ribs. I've really been banged up in this business in thirty-five years. But when you're young, you don't mind so much. Put a piece of tape on it, go out and do it again. So we were the stunt co-ordinators on *She-Gods*. We fooled around and had a good time. It was really a great location and when I think back on it I think of the two pictures together.

Q: So after that, and maybe because of what Beverly Garland said, Roger gave you the lead in *Rock All Night*.

MILLER: I'm not giving her too much credit. I think Roger saw something there. I remember a lot about *Rock*

All Night. See, I remember it *because* it was my first starring role. It was the first time it said "Dick Miller starring in ..." and it was great! But once that was out of the way, to me it was just a bigger part. More words to learn. I had a fight scene at the beginning of the picture. And I get carried out under this guy's arm. Burt Nelson. He was a big guy and his girl friend had given him this gold chain. It was about a two foot chain because he was a big guy. I put my arm through it and straightened it out into a piece of wire. He held that chain and it was straight up, like a hanger. "My God," he said, "what did you do?" You don't wear fancy jewelry when you're doing fight scenes.

Q: After *Rock All Night* you starred in *War of the Satellites* and *A Bucket of Blood.* But you turned down the lead in *The Little Shop of Horrors.* Why?

MILLER: They wanted me to do the same picture all over again. I said, "Bullshit. I just did that." I didn't want to do the same part again. Youthful, artistic integrity. I just said, off the top of my head, "Give it to Jonathan." I told Roger I'd do something else in the picture.

Q: Did you pick the part or did the part pick you?

MILLER: What do you mean by that?

Q: Did you read the script and see a part you liked or ...?

MILLER: Oh. No. No. No. I said, "Let's see what's in there. What else am I right for?" I didn't want to just walk in and buy some flowers and walk out. But I wasn't thinking of the size of the part. In my mind (and this wasn't very astute, business-wise) I didn't think about the fact that I'd just done a pretty good picture, and I'd done a couple back-to-back that I starred in, and I should continue in that vein. It didn't occur to me that if I took a secondary role, just a featured spot, that I'd be cutting my career at that point. For years I thought back to what a stupid career move that was. But I did it and I have to live with it. What it did was cut my career as a star. And then another starring role came along and I did the same thing on that: *Stakeout on Dope Street.* I just walked out of the picture. I didn't want to work on weekends. Jonathan told me that when I quit, the three leads were moved up. He had a small part and they moved him into one of the leads. That cost me a lot of work too. The people who made that wound up doing a bunch of TV series later on in life and would never use me because they thought I had walked off the picture. What they didn't know was when I walked off Roger asked if I was walking off because it was a bad picture. I said, "No. I think it's a good picture. I think you should go ahead and make it." It was pretty much my final say that got them the financing to do that picture. But since I didn't know these guys were mad at me, I thought it was just a matter of artistic difference. It took me seven or eight years to find out (a guy named Al Kallis told me) they were pissed off at me because I walked off the picture.

Q: Getting back to *Little Shop*: you took the role of the flower eater. And

you shot for two days?

MILLER: Little Shop was basically done in two days. They like to say it was done in two days and a night but they did a couple of nights shooting on it.

Q: Were you there the whole time or did you just come in for your scenes?

MILLER: No. We were there. We didn't know when we were going to work. We shot in sequence, you know. It was the easiest way to go because everybody was there. And it was all taking place on one set. So all of that stuff in the shop ... We went right through it. It would have made no sense to go back and forth with the structure that we had there. Maybe they doubled up on the three girls that came in and asked for flowers.

Maybe they got that stuff even though it was here and there. But most of it was shot pretty much in sequence. Pretty much. It wouldn't have made any sense to bounce around.

Q: When you did that picture, I'm sure you had no idea that it would develop the kind of following it did.

MILLER: Of course not. Only Frank Capra ever said I think we're gonna

Barboura O'Neil (aka Barboura Morris) and Dick Miller in Confessions of a Sorority Girl.

have a winner here. You know. Tell Jimmy it's all right to buy that ranch. This one'll run for forty years. We made a picture that was meant to be a second half (or third half) of a bill at a bad drive-in someplace and that was it. It was made for nothing, and again it was the old Corman format of using a standing set. That's how *The Terror* was made, you know,

Dick Miller thought he was a little short to be the hero of War of the Satellites, *but a gun is always a good equalizer. Here Dick has the drop on Richard Devon.*

which is the classic of all classics.

Q: The reviews of *Little Shop* were favorable.

MILLER: I gotta admit, although nobody said this is gonna be a cult film, or this will be such and such, the reviews did kind of indicate that it was something special. This is a sneaky little cheap film that was made that's

kind of funny, it's got this off beat humor in it and if you can understand that you're gonna love it. This was the general trend of the reviews. The reviewers saw something in it. They saw the humor in it. I don't know if Roger ever saw the humor. I don't know if he ever understood it. But he went along with it. And even though they say he may not have the best sense of humor (and it's true, I don't think he has) he was open enough to go along with it because *we* said it was funny. And he bought it.

Q: It was a more obvious comedy than *A Bucket of Blood*.

MILLER: Bucket of Blood wasn't meant as a satire or a slapstick comedy. It was meant to be dark humor. It was a very serious story. The only comedy in it was pretty much the attitude that I adopted. It was a strange part. I was playing a mental retard basically, and a murderer, and the only way to make these pieces pay off was to adopt a certain attitude and that became humorous. I think I played it intentionally that way, I don't think it was an accidental performance. I wanted more of the innocence and naivety of the character. I didn't want him to be a stark killer or a moronic killer, I wanted him to be an innocent killer. And I think that's where the humor came from. But it was basically a very straight story. It's an old French classic. It's nothing new. It's been done many times. *House of Wax* and things of that nature. *Little Shop of Horrors* was intentionally humorous. And mostly because everybody's attitude was: Let's have a ball. Let's make a movie.

Q: How do you feel about the picture? Was it just another film off the assembly line?

MILLER: Okay. The picture got made and it got this strange response and it did business and then it started to play. Today everybody makes a movie and if it bombs they call it a cult film. They say there's hidden things in it that you don't see. To me that's bullshit. A cult film has to develop a cult. And you don't do that in the second year after it fails. We kept hearing it was showing here and there and the college kids were eating it up. This was five years after the thing was made. Normally we had a life run of six months on most of our pictures. You made it, you got as much money as you could out of it, and then it became, you know, mandolin picks. There was very little you could do with those films, which is why Roger never copyrighted them. That's why he almost lost the whole deal when they wanted to make it into a musical. 'Cause he didn't think these things would ever go anyplace. A lot of the films are lost. We don't even know who has them anymore. *Sorority Girl*. I never saw that picture again. Never came back. A lot of them just disappeared. But this was a picture that somehow, a year after, we were hearing about it. Not because *we* said it was a cult film but because places like the Nuart started showing it. Then it was five years later and we were talkin' about it: You know they're still showing that little picture we made. Remember that thing? College kids would come up and say, "You know we show this picture every year." Later you're not only hearing it from the California universities, but from places like Oskosh and Kansas and Utah. Silly places are playing this film. Suddenly, it's ten years later and you're still hearing about the damn film. It won't go away. It's like the crud. You can't get rid of it. And *that* was my attitude. I never took it anymore seriously than that. Every time it would come up I'd say, "Yeah, we made that picture. But did you see *Bucket of Blood*?" I couldn't understand why they didn't realize what a classic little film *it* was. Then I started getting reports on that from Europe. The capper was when Arkoff or Nicholson or somebody went to New York City when the Museum of Modern Art there asked for a copy of *A Bucket of Blood* for their archives. Every major movie museum in the world has a copy of *A Bucket of Blood*. That is one of their prime attractions. Something they want to keep for all time. So I was amazed that this country, except in a certain area, hadn't eaten it up like they did *A Little Shop of Horrors*. But *Little Shop of Horrors* would keep turning up.

Q: I think if *Bucket of Blood* had had more money in it ...

MILLER: That's what I've always said. I thought it was a classic picture in every way except the money. Some of the effects were cheats. If they'd only had some production money. Everybody's good. The story's good. They would screw up on things that wouldn't get laughs, but then they would show a mannequin and say it was statue. Things like that. And they cheated a little on the end. They couldn't do what they wanted to do.

Q: What did they want to do?

MILLER: I'm supposed to be covered in clay and things like that. It would have been a more startling effect than some gray make-up. I never said there's something wrong here, there's something wrong there.

Q: Did you see the new *Little Shop of Horrors*?

MILLER: Yes I did. I resisted going first run.

Q: Had you seen the play?

MILLER: No. There was some controversy about the play. Jackie Joseph called me up and said they didn't invite her to the play. Jonathan had to buy his own tickets to go see the play. Jackie got invited by some publicity lady friend of hers. I thought they were a bunch of assholes. I said, "How could they have made this play and not invited us?" They said, "We've got West Coast people handling it now, it's not the people that created the Broadway show, and they don't know who you are." Well, that's garbage. I was pretty pissed off at the show and I didn't want to go. Then the picture came out. My attitude then was that it was a big joke. I said, "Yeah. I'll go see it." And I was really wishing them luck. I wasn't hoping the picture would bomb. I couldn't understand why they went to England to do it or any of that. My comment on it afterwards was that it was like watching eighty minutes of rubber lips.

Q: They spent twenty-six million on theirs and you spent thirty-six thousand on yours.

MILLER: That's a fair appraisal. Nobody knows what the figures really are, but that's close enough to be valid. Ours has lasted 30 years. Let's see how long theirs lasts.

Q: You told me you were up for the lead role in *Machine Gun Kelly.* Why didn't you get it?

MILLER: Charles Bronson was a nobody at that time. He'd been playing heavies. This could cause a little dissension but, what the hell, I'll tell you the story anyway. Bobby Campbell was writing the script. Bobby was supposed to be a very good friend of mine. He had some strange thinking. And he had some strange loyalties. For him to want his brother to do the part is not a strange loyalty. That to me makes a lot of sense. But Roger told him to write the picture for me and he wrote it another way. He went to New York and started sending telegrams and making phone calls to Jim Nicholson (who told me this years later, after he and Arkoff broke up), saying I was wrong for the part. The only person that could do it was Billy Campbell. It's about an Irish killer (I don't know if Kelly was even Irish; it could have been a made-up name). Everybody was German in those days. Dutch Schultz wasn't German. He wasn't Dutch either. Arkoff hit the ceiling. He said it was bullshit. And he told Roger ... Now I may have this backwards. I don't know who told who. But the three principals involved

were Arkoff, Nicholson, and Roger. Somebody said, "This is bullshit. I can't stand it. Get me the names of people who could play this part. I don't want to see Billy's name on it and I don't want to see Dick's name on it." And they came up with Charlie. They called me and they paid me off. I thought about it many times. I walked away from a lot of parts but this one walked away from me and I really wanted it. Dick Miller as Machine Gun Kelly. I think it would have done for me the same thing it did for Charlie.

Q: I just recently saw *Carnival Rock* for the first time.

MILLER: I liked *Carnival Rock.* It was a good little picture. Probably more funny things happened with *Carnival Rock* than any picture I can remember.

Q: Tell me.

MILLER: Well, we had David Stewart on that. Roger said, "We're getting a Tony Award-winner to come out from Broadway. It's the Blue Angel story, to clarify this: the old man falls in love with the young girl; his buddy tells him that she's no good for him. I was supposed to play the part of her young boyfriend. I read it and said, "This is no part." Roger said, "Well, you can't do the old man." I said, "I could do his friend." He said, "You're too young to do his friend." I said, "How about we change it a little." One line covered it, at my suggestion. Instead of the character being a lifelong friend I changed it so that I was someone that he practically adopted. I wandered off the streets when I was fourteen years old and have been with him for twenty years. Like a father and son relationship instead of a brother relationship. David Stewart proceeded on the first day to slap me. He turned to Roger and said, "You know, I felt like – since he is my son, sort of – I want to hit him." Roger said, "That's a good idea." The guy hauled off and slapped me. I said, "Hey. What are you doin'?" First of all, this was in rehearsal. Roger said, "We decided we were going to hit you." I said, "First of all, this is pictures.

"Most people don't like to go to the dentist," Wilbur tells Seymour. "But I rather enjoy it myself, don't you? There's a real feeling of growth, of progress when that old drill goes in."

You don't have to hit me. You can miss me by a foot and it's gonna look good. Probably look better." We rehearsed it a few times and David Stewart said, "I don't feel it." So Roger said, "The guy's a Tony Award-winner. He wants to make physical contact, otherwise he doesn't feel it. Can he hit you on the take? Just one take where he hits you." I said, "Okay. But this is wrong. It's not gonna look right." By then I'd done enough fights in pictures to know what looked good and what didn't. He hauled off and whacked me on the take, right across my ear. I tell ya, I had a ringing in my ear for six months after that. It looked so bad they couldn't use it anyway. And there's a big cut. You see him say something and in the next scene I'm

standing with my tie up around my neck and you wonder what happened to my tie. What Roger didn't know about David Stewart (and Roger was really terrified of the guy) was that he had won his Tony Award for playing – in Camino Real – a homosexual. Had nothing to do with great acting ability or even the part. That's like letting Gene Autry do Lear. You know. And this guy used to do all this running around; all this "method" crap. He'd do push-ups before a take. Or he'd run around the studio. There was a scene where I was supposed to pull him away from this dressing room door and he kept pulling the knob off. And they'd hammer the knob back on and they would very patiently say, "Doorknob's not real, Mr. Stewart. Don't pull the doorknob off. Don't try and turn it. *Make believe* you're turning it." Never had that concept. And I'm supposed to pull him away from the door and slam him into the other wall and say, "Leave her alone. She's no good for you. She's a young girl. Leave her alone." She's in there with her boyfriend. He wouldn't let go of the doorknob. I'm trying to pull him and the guy outweighed me by seventy or eighty pounds. I couldn't move him. Terrible things happened. He kept banging his head every time I slammed him against the wall. One of the grips or somebody came over there and hammered one of those two-headed nails into the wall, just where his head hit. I asked them about it later and they said they'd done it on purpose because they were tired of the guy. He'd been there two days

and he was driving them crazy with his method acting. They couldn't get a shot. He had to run around the stage so he could breathe hard. I figured the only way to drag him across the room was to sink my fingers in and pull. Two days later he showed me his arm. It was all purple and green. I said, "Gee, I'm sorry." And he said, "It's all right. I used the pain." When his head hit the wall on that last take I saw blood trickling down his neck. That nail had caught him on the side of the head. I said, "You're bleeding." He said, "I can use that pain. I felt something was wrong." Method acting! He was doing a scene with Jonathan where he was supposed to see the girl with her boyfriend and have a heart attack. He gave Jonathan a straight pin and told him, "When I turn my head, stick me in the leg with that pin." When Jonathan told me I said, "What, are you kidding?" He said, "What should I do?" I said, "Stick the friggin' pin in him." They played the scene. Jonathan jabbed the pin into the guy and they had to come over with pliers to pull the pin out. As it turned out David Stewart was terrible in the part. He was atrocious. Now there's a follow-up to this. I find myself doing "McCloud" a couple of years later. I'm working with one of the finest actors in the business: Joseph Wiseman. Marvelous. Brilliant actor. He may be one of the ten best in the business. We're shooting on the Universal lot at night and we start talkin' and the name comes up – David Stewart. And I said, "I gotta tell you about this guy" and I proceeded to tell him the same story I just told you about this idiot, this moron, this asshole, this imbecile. I go on and on and he said, "You know David Stewart is dead." I said, "Oh, really? Tough. That's the way it goes." (It turned out that David Stewart had died of a heart attack, three or four months prior to this night.) Wiseman looks at me and said, "David Stewart was my dearest friend." I felt like crap. It influenced my performance. Not that it was anything too in-depth. I felt awful all night long. We finished shooting. Sun came up. We went back to the trailers to change. Wiseman offered me a ride. I got into the car and said, "Joseph I really have to apologize. I don't really know how to say it ..." He said, "I don't know how to say *this* but – I don't know who David Stewart is!"

Q: So bring me up to date. How did "Fame" happen?

MILLER: They called me for *a* part, as usual. They had a bad character who was really a *bad* character. A step above a child molester. Ran a local saloon and bowling alley. And he had a crush on this little seventeen-year-old. I played it for laughs. I figured it was a little heavy. It had some funny scenes written into it but I decided to play the whole thing that way. They called me back. They liked the character. It's the kind of thing you dream of. You do a guest shot on a TV show and they want to bring you back. That was around Christmas. Only they changed it. I still had the bowling alley but not the saloon. It was a pizza and coke joint. No booze because MGM didn't want it. And they liked that

show so they wrote me into three or four more shows that season. They told me they'd be bringing me back the next year but I sweated it out just like anybody else. The next year I did around ten shows. Then they gave me a contract and I did twenty-two segments. And now the show is in the toilet, it was the best experience I've had in the business in years. I was a fan of the show before I got on it. I would never miss "Fame." I never saw that kind of work done in an hour show. They were putting on a little MGM musical every week. When I got on the show I was even more amazed because I saw how much effort and energy went into the shows. They work hard.

Q: What was the shooting schedule for an episode?

MILLER: Seven days.

Q: Like the old days.

MILLER: Yeah. They turned out ... Well, not quite an hour. Forty-eight minutes or something. Whatever it was, they were turning out that show every single week. And there was always one major production number. And usually two or three extra songs were in there with a little dancing added. It's a shame it went off the air because there's nothing like it on TV. The show's been in the black continuously. The fact is they were making the show for less money than they were selling them for. The show had a budget of a million dollars and they were turning it out for nine hundred thousand so the show was a hundred thousand in profit right off the bat. So there was no reason to dump it.

Lorimar bought the lot. They wanted all the MGM shows off the lot. They particularly wanted the sound stages we were using which were the two biggest stages on the lot to do "Knots Landing." To move a show for one season you'd lose money. It takes almost a million dollars to tear down the sets and move them to another lot. In fact, one of the reasons they gave me a contract was because they wanted to know if they should keep my set. Because it cost them thirty thousand dollars every time they put it up and took it down. They said, "If we have you under contract we'll make it a permanent set." 'Cause I was giving them a bad time. They'd ask if I could work the next two shows and I'd tell them I didn't know because I was doing a picture. In fact, I was turning down anything bigger than one or two day job pictures because I really thought "Fame" was important. Joe Dante called me to do *Innerspace* and I said I couldn't do it. I knew it would pay me good money but I didn't want to give up "Fame." I didn't have a contract at the time, so I started telling the "Fame" people that I had to do this picture and that picture. I put a little pressure on them and they finally gave me a contract. I was very disappointed that the show wasn't renewed even though I knew in my heart it wasn't gonna be picked up. You can overcome a lot of obstacles but when a studio wants you off their lot, and you can't get a guarantee for at least two more seasons ...

Q: So what now?

MILLER: Now I don't know. Now it's a matter of sitting and waiting and like every actor from Laurence Olivier down you think you'll never work again. But something'll come up.

FILMOGRAPHY
(As Performer)

1955

Apache Woman
American Releasing Corporation
Screenplay by Lou Rusoff
Produced and Directed by Roger Corman

1956

Gunslinger
American Releasing Corporation
Screenplay by Charles B. Griffith and Mark Hanna
Produced and Directed by Roger Corman

Oklahoma Woman
American Releasing Corporation
Screenplay by Lou Rusoff
Produced and Directed by Roger Corman

It Conquered the World
American International
Screenplay by Lou Rusoff and (uncredited) Charles B. Griffith
Produced and Directed by Roger Corman

1957

Sorority Girl (a.k.a. Confessions of a Sorority Girl)
American International
Screenplay by Leo Lieberman
Produced and Directed by Roger Corman

Carnival Rock Howco International
Screenplay by Leo Lieberman
Produced and Directed by
Roger Corman

Naked Paradise (a.k.a.
Thunder Over Hawaii)
American International
Screenplay by Charles B. Griffith,
Mark Hanna, and (uncredited)
R. Wright Campbell
Produced and Directed by
Roger Corman

Not of This Earth Allied Artists
Screenplay by Charles B. Griffith
and Mark Hanna
Produced and Directed by
Roger Corman

Rock All Night
American International
Screenplay by Charles B. Griffith
based on "The Little Guy"
Produced and Directed by
Roger Corman

The Undead
American International
Screenplay by Charles B. Griffith
and Mark Hanna
Produced and Directed by
Roger Corman

War of the Satellites Allied Artists
Screenplay by
Lawrence Louis Goldman
Produced and Directed by
Roger Corman

1959

A Bucket of Blood
American International
Screenplay by Charles B. Griffith

Produced and Directed by
Roger Corman

1962

The Premature Burial
American International
Screenplay by Charles Beaumont
and Ray Russell *based on the story
by* Edgar Allan Poe
Produced and Directed by
Roger Corman

1963

The Terror Filmgroup/
American International
Screenplay by Leo Gordon and
Jack Hill
Produced by Roger Corman
Directed by Roger Corman and
(uncredited) Francis Ford Coppola,
Jack Hill, and Monte Hellman

1966

The Wild Angels
American International
Screenplay by Charles B. Griffith
Produced and Directed by
Roger Corman

1967

The St. Valentine's Day Massacre
20th-Century Fox
Screenplay by Howard Browne
Produced and Directed by
Roger Corman

The Trip American International
Screenplay by Jack Nicholson
Produced and Directed by
Roger Corman

Executive Action
National General

Screenplay by Dalton Trumbo
Produced by Edward Lewis
Directed by David Miller

Fly Me New World
Screenplay by Miller Drake
Produced and Directed by
Cirio Santiago

1974

Darktown Strutters New World
Screenplay by George Armitage
Produced and Directed by
William Witney

Teenage Models
(a.k.a. ***Game Show Models***)
Independent-International
Written, Produced and Directed by
David Neil Gottlieb

Big Bad Mama New World
Screenplay by William Norton
and Francis Doel
Produced by Roger Corman
Directed by Steve Carver

Candy Stripe Nurses New World
Produced by Julie Corman
Written and Directed by Allan Holleb

1975

Summer School Teachers
New World
Produced by Julie Corman
Written and Directed by
Barbara Peters

Capone 20th-Century Fox
Screenplay by Howard Browne
Produced by Roger Corman
Directed by Steve Carver

"I'm going to recommend you to all my friends," Wilbur Force tells Seymour.

Courtesy Mark Thomas McGee Collection

1976

Cannonball New World
Screenplay by Paul Bartel
and Donald C. Simpson
Produced by Sam Felfman
Directed by Paul Bartel

Hollywood Boulevard New World
Screenplay by Patrick Hobby
Produced by Jon Davidson
Directed by Joe Dante and
Allan Arkush

1978

Piranha New World
Screenplay by John Sayles
Produced by Jon Davidson
Directed by Joe Dante

1979

Rock 'n' Roll High School
New World
Screenplay by Richard Whitley,
Russ Dvonch and Joseph McBride
Produced by Michael Finnell
Directed by Allan Arkush

1981

The Howling Avco Embassy
Screenplay by John Sayles
and Terence H. Winkless
Produced by Michael Finnell
and Jack Conrad
Directed by Joe Dante

1983

Twilight Zone – The Movie
Warner Brothers
Screenplay by Richard Matheson,
George Clayton Johnson, Josh
Rogan and John Landis
Produced by Steven Spielberg

and John Landis
Directed by John Landis, Joe Dante,
Steven Spielberg and George Miller

Get Crazy Avco Embassy
Screenplay by Danny Opatoshu,
Henry Rosenbaum, and David Taylor
Produced by Hunt Lowry
Directed by Allan Arkush

Heart Like a Wheel
20th-Century Fox
Written, Produced and Directed by
Jonathan Kaplan

1984

The Terminator Orion
Screenplay by James Cameron
and Gale Anne Hurd
Produced by Gale Anne Hurd
Directed by James Cameron

Gremlins Warner Brothers
Screenplay by Christopher Columbus
Produced by Michael Finnell
Directed by Joe Dante

1985

Explorers Paramount
Screenplay by Eric Luke
Produced by Edward S. Feldman
and David Bombyk
Directed by Joe Dante

1987

Innerspace Warner Brothers
Screenplay by Jeffrey Boam
and Chip Proser
Produced by Michael Finnell
Directed by Joe Dante

(As Writer)

1970

Which Way to the Front?
Warner Brothers
Screenplay by Gerald Gardner
and Dee Caruso *from a story by*
Gerald Gardner and Dick Miller
Produced and Directed by Jerry Lewis

1974

T.T.T. Jackson New World
Screenplay by Dick Miller
and Ken Metcalf
Produced and Directed by
Cirio Santiago

CHARLES B. GRIFFITH
(The Writer)

ALTHOUGH FRENCH FILM CRITICS would have us believe the director is always a film's author (a notion many directors encourage until things go sour and then they willingly go back to being hired hands), it seems clear that the "auteur" of *The Little Shop* is its writer, Chuck Griffith. It's logical to assume that a two day feature,

Dr. Farb becomes just another meal for Audrey Junior.

shot with multiple cameras, wouldn't leave much room for creative direction or camera work. That leaves the performers and the writer to take care of business.

Charles Byron Griffith was born in Chicago to a show business family. His father was in vaudeville, his grandfather was a circus tightrope walker, and his mother and grandmother were the leads on the "Myrt and Marge" radio soap opera. And Griffith wanted to be a part of that. During his high school years in a military academy he sold poetry, structured to allow room for the insertion of any young lady's name, to his fellow cadettes. When he was nineteen he came to Hollywood and tried his hand at screenwriting. He was living with his grandmother at the time. She got him an agent, but seven screenplays later Griffith still hadn't sold anything. Through one of the agent's connections Griffith met Roger Corman, who needed a script for a film he was planning to make in Portugal. Ultimately the deal fell through but Griffith had his foot in the door now. Corman knew Griffith could write quickly, and hired him to write a western, *The Girls of Hangtown Mesa*, but Griffith wrote his screenplay without giving any thought to the budget. Corman gave him a lesson in economics before asking him to write another western, *Gunslinger*.

GRIFFITH: He took me to a Randolph Scott western called *Three Hours to Kill* and told me to write the same picture, only change the sheriff's part to a woman. That was one of Roger's favorite tricks: take a story and change

the lead from a male to a female.

Q: I don't think Randolph Scott ever made a picture called *Three Hours to Kill*.

GRIFFITH: Really?

Q: Dana Andrews made a picture with that title but not Randolph Scott.

GRIFFITH: God! I've been telling that story for years. Well, it was a Randolph Scott western and Roger was going to shoot for three days at Ingram's Ranch in Topanga Canyon. (It's a mobile home park now.) It had a town street with a few acres of scrub around it. The usual bullshit. And the other three days were going to be shot out at Iverson's Ranch out past Chatsworth. So I went out to Ingram's and copied the names off the signs to use for the character's names. That way they wouldn't have to re-do the signs. By then I knew where Roger was at. And I had a look around the land and I figured out that if you looked this way and that you could write the exteriors of the whole picture there and save thirty minutes a day each way, which was a whole shooting day on a six day picture. Roger was delighted. We shot the whole thing at Ingram's. That was going to be the last six day picture. It went seven. Roger was very bitter.

Q: I heard it rained every day.

GRIFFITH: It wasn't a bad rain. We didn't use lights anyway, just reflectors. And there was nothing to reflect so it was all subtle. It actually gave the picture a more interesting look.

Q: How did you feel about being asked to copy someone else's movie?

GRIFFITH: When I grew up, the

ethics of *The Red Shoes* were predominant. You remember the scene in the early part of the picture when Julian Krasner has gone to the concert and heard his music being performed as written by his own professor? The professor had ripped it off. And he goes to the impresario who had hired him and the impresario said: "Remember, it's much more satisfying to be stolen from than to have to steal." Those were the ethics that I grew up with and not until 1963 did I run into an opposite ethic when I met Mike Reeves. Michael Reeves was a very intense young man who came to Italy to make a picture for Paul Maslanski which I wrote in three days. Mike was very ambitious. His idol was Don Siegel, whom I'd never heard of. He knew every shot of every picture that Don Siegel had ever done and was about to duplicate them. I said, "What do you want to do that for?" "Well, these are marvelous," he said. I'm hearing buff talk for the first time. When I was a kid there were no films to be buffs about. Films were, to our eyes, improving by leaps and bounds all of the time. The films of the thirties were archaic in the forties and so on, and they reached some kind of technical plateau in the sixties as far as straight filmmaking. But for anybody to copy Hitchcock's set-ups or Don Siegel's (whoever he was) set-ups was a great mystery to me. We had a big fight about day for night. I'd shot second unit on this picture called *Revenge of the Blood Beast*. Mel Welles was in it and a lot of other friends. It was about Communist

Transylvania. It was a comedy and they took all the comedy out of it. They got cold feet at the last minute. I even shot a great comedy car chase between the van and the old yellow car that Van Helsing was driving. Anyway, Mike had been told by some big name cameraman that you shoot day for night with the sun at your back and heavily under-exposed. I told him the guy was pulling his leg. We both shot completely opposite day for night techniques on that picture. He shot it that way and it looked sort of like newsreel shots from the concentration camps. It had that quality. And I shot Hollywood style day for night which is, of course, directly into the light. But Mike was a real nice guy. He was the first person to tell me that *Little Shop of Horrors* was a cult film. He brought with him from England some clippings from British film magazines that were raving on and on and on about *Bucket of Blood*, saying it was the first genuine black comedy to come out of America and all that ignorant talk and they'd heard about *Little Shop of Horrors*, that it was supposed to be better, but they hadn't seen it yet. I thought: What on earth is going on? Mike called me from London later to tell me *Little Shop* was on television. This was about '65. Until then, I didn't even know the picture had been released. I left a few months after it was made.

Q: Where did you go?

GRIFFITH: I tried to make an Arab-Israeli war picture here right after *Little Shop of Horrors*. Mel Welles and I had a company. For eleven thousand we were trying to do this war picture in color out by the Salton Sea. We were picketed by the unions. They shut us down. I had some Israeli friends here who said, "Let's finish the picture in Israel." We had to start over again. I went off on a boat with my Volkswagen, to Israel, dead broke. I arrived there sort of a ward of the state. We had twenty-nine thousand feet of short-ends that we were going to sell but when we got there it was all fogged. My lawyer didn't send me the money to leave, so I was stranded. I was living on a rooftop. I had a good time there. Two years.

Q: Is that why you weren't involved in any of the Edgar Allan Poe pictures? That would be about the time that Roger was making those.

GRIFFITH: I was willing, but Roger wanted to upgrade his product. And I was cheap. I came on the set of *House of Usher.* That was where I first met Mark Damon and Vincent Price. I saw all this stuff like cobwebs and rubber cement. Things I'd been asking for for years. The most technical we ever got was on *The Undead* with a few B-smokers and cobwebs. Roger didn't hire me to do a Poe picture until we were in Europe. It was *The Gold Bug.* It was *Little Shop of Horrors* again. I spent a long time on it. Peter Lorre, Vincent Price, and Basil Rathbone were supposed to star in that. Can't you see me having a good time writing for those guys? Wonderful. Price was the southern planter who's mansion had been burned out and it was just a ruin but he was still living in it to try to keep up appear-

ances. Rathbone was an English carpetbagger who was coming to clean everybody out. Lorre was the servant in the house. His uncle was an admiral in the Transylvanian navy. So I told Price, "You show Basil Rathbone the paintings of your ancestors on the wall." He said, "Oh, no, not again!" And I said, "Wait. Wait. They're all famous paintings. Like Blueboy. And you're trying to pass them off as your ancestors." "Oh. I get it. You have to have The Laughing Cavalier." So I added The Laughing Cavalier. 'Cause at the end he says, "Here's my mother. Don't you think she has an enigmatic smile?" That was a lot of fun. The Gold Bug was a little bug that lived in a snuff box that Lorre had and it would dance on the keys of the harpsichord at night, doing the Gold Bug rag. And if it bit people it turned them into gold. And always in positions like The White Rock ad; the maid reaching into the water. And the one-armed bandit. Lots of those. And Price tries to melt them down and they turn back into flesh. So you see the parallel with *The Little Shop of Horrors* and *Bucket of Blood* plot. He's trying to unload the gold statues. There's Auntie Bellum, the maid whose feet squeak. They think her shoes squeak but when she's barefooted her feet squeak. "Sometimes I squeak, sometimes I doesn't," she says. But Lorre died while I was writing the script. Right in the middle of it. And I had to finish that script for him. And it was over three hundred pages. In the sixties all my scripts were coming out over three hundred pages. There was going to be another comedy after *Little Shop* called *Gluttony*, about the owner of a restaurant that serves up people, but cannibalism was against the code at the time so we dropped it.

Q: But you did make *Creature From the Haunted Sea*?

GRIFFITH: Yes, but that wasn't planned as one of the group. Roger was in Puerto Rico making something and he needed another script. That was another version of *Naked Paradise*. We did four versions of *Naked Paradise*.

Q: That was the one he filmed in Hawaii. Did you get to go?

GRIFFITH: I pleaded to go, but no.

Q: I always figured that movie was made as an excuse to take a vacation.

GRIFFITH: There's no time for a vacation on a schedule like that. Remember, Roger was still making ten day pictures then.

Q: You said there were *four* versions?

GRIFFITH: That's right. *Beast from Haunted Cave* was the second one. The original picture was about the robbery of a sugar plantation. Before

That's writer Charles Byron Griffith holding a gun to Mushnik's nose. Griffith also supplied the voice of Audrey Junior.

the criminals could get away in their boat a storm moved in. I simply transported the story from Hawaii to South Dakota and had the criminals snowed in before they could get away with the gold they'd stolen from one of the mines. Everything was the same. Except Roger wanted a monster. So

I kept the monster in a cave where it couldn't interfere with anything. *Atlas* was the fourth version. I wanted to call it *Atlas, the Guided Muscle* but Roger wouldn't go for it.

Q: *Naked Paradise* was on a double bill with *Flesh and the Spur* which was written by you and Mark Hanna. But that one wasn't for Corman. How did that come about?

GRIFFITH: AIP told Mark Hanna and he told me, as I vaguely recall. I was glad to be doing a job for somebody else, 'cause I thought they might be more painstaking in the material.

Q: But wasn't American International's approach to picture-making pretty much the same as Corman's?

GRIFFITH: Yeah. Jim Nicholson and Sam Arkoff went on the assumption that on their budgets they could not make good pictures. They made saturation product that was in and out in five days. Skim it off the top and run, over and over again.

Q: What were they like?

GRIFFITH: Sam was very straightforward and witty. Jim was a phoney from beginning to end. Big smile. He was the good cop and Sam was the bad cop. Jim would make the deal and offer you a million and then Sam would come in and get it down to what they really wanted. I never trusted Jim because I thought he was too friendly. A false teeth smile. I had nothing

Gunslinger was Charles Griffith's version of an old Randolph Scott western. Beverly Garland took the Scott role. John Ireland was the heavy.

against him personally. We got along fine, better than I did with Sam. But I didn't believe him.

Q: *Flesh and the Spur* had a spur fight in it which was pretty unusual.

GRIFFITH: In *Gunslinger* it was pitchforks. I was ripe for that kind of gore, but I won't do it now.

Q: Why?

GRIFFITH: I just think it's ugly.

Q: Is that why you don't want your daughter to see horror pictures?

GRIFFITH: I know how traumatic they can be. When I was twelve I went to see *The Mad Ghoul* and *The Son of Frankenstein*. They were scary. At the time I didn't see the flaws. I wasn't looking for the flaws. I came back and I couldn't sleep. Absolutely terrified. I threw up on the floor. Made a nuisance of myself. I wouldn't go to any more horror pictures until I started writing them.

Q: Which did you like better: *Bucket of Blood* or *Little Shop*?

GRIFFITH: I used to like *Bucket of Blood* but now I think *Little Shop* is the better of the two.

Q: Why?

GRIFFITH: It's the one audiences seem to respond to. It's the one they seem to like.

Q: How did you come to be the voice of the plant?

GRIFFITH: I stood off camera and read the lines just to give the actors something to respond to. Roger was going to dub another voice in later. But it got laughs so he decided to leave it the way it was. I also play the thief who comes to rob the store and gets eaten by the plant. My father was in the picture. So was my grand-mother. A lot of my relatives were in it. I got a big kick out of the *Time* review, of the show in New York, that talked about me. The show didn't give me any credit. They tried to hide the fact that I was involved because I was suing them. The review helped.

A few years back Griffith had a sequel in mind to *Little Shop* which completely disregarded the climax of the original picture. Seymour isn't dead a quarter of a century later, but rather he's in hiding, growing another plant. Gravis Mushnik has become the bloom tycoon he always wanted to be with a shop in Beverly Hills and married to Audrey. Will Griffith ever get this project off the ground (or should we say out of skid row and into Beverly Hills)? We'll just have to wait and see.

FILMOGRAPHY
(As Writer)

1956

Gunslinger
American Releasing Corporation
Screenplay by Charles B. Griffith and Mark Hanna
Produced and Directed by Roger Corman

It Conquered the World
American International
Screenplay by Lou Rusoff and (uncredited) Charles B. Griffith
Produced and Directed by Roger Corman

1957

Teenage Doll Allied Artists
Screenplay by Charles B. Griffith
Produced and Directed by Roger Corman

Flesh and the Spur
American International
Screenplay by Charles B. Griffith and Mark Hanna
Produced by Alex Gordon
Directed by Edward L. Cahn

Naked Paradise
(a.k.a. **Thunder Over Hawaii**)
American International
Screenplay by Charles B. Griffith, Mark Hanna, and (uncredited) R. Wright Campbell
Produced and Directed by Roger Corman

Not of This Earth Allied Artists
Screenplay by Charles B. Griffith and Mark Hanna
Produced and Directed by Roger Corman

Rock All Night
American International
Screenplay by Charles B. Griffith based on "The Little Guy"
Produced and Directed by Roger Corman

The Undead American International
Screenplay by Charles B. Griffith and Mark Hanna
Produced and Directed by Roger Corman

Attack of the Crab Monsters
Allied Artists
Screenplay by Charles B. Griffith

"FEEEEEED

Courtesy Mark Thomas McGee Collection

MEEEEEEE!"

Produced and Directed by
Roger Corman

1958

Ghost of the China Sea Columbia
Written and Produced by
Charles B. Griffith
Directed by Fred F. Sears

Forbidden Island Columbia
Written, Produced and Directed by
Charles B. Griffith

1959

A Bucket of Blood
American International
Screenplay by Charles B. Griffith
Produced and Directed by
Roger Corman

1960

Beast From the Haunted Cave
Filmgroup
Screenplay by Charles B. Griffith
Produced by Gene Corman
Directed by Monte Hellman

John Agar, Marla English and Touch (Michael) Connors from Flesh and the Spur, *written by Charles Griffith.*

Ski Troop Attack Filmgroup
Screenplay by Charles B. Griffith
Produced and Directed by
Roger Corman

Creature From the Haunted Sea
Filmgroup
Screenplay by Charles B. Griffith
Produced and Directed by
Roger Corman

1961

Atlas Filmgroup
Screenplay by Charles B. Griffith
Produced and Directed by
Roger Corman

1966

The Wild Angels
American International
Screenplay by Charles B. Griffith
Produced and Directed by
Roger Corman

1967

Devil's Angels
American International
Screenplay by Charles B. Griffith
Produced by Burt Topper
Directed by Daniel Haller

1968

Barbarella Paramount
Screenplay by (among others)
Terry Southern, Roger Vadim, Jean-Claude Forest, Vittorio Bonicelli, Brian Degas, Claude Brule, Tudor Gates, Clement Biddlewood, Charles B. Griffith and The Mormon Tabernacle Choir
Produced by Dino De Laurentiis
Directed by Roger Vadim

1974

Death Race 2000 New World
Screenplay by Robert Thom and
Charles Griffith *from a story by*
Ib Melchior
Produced by Roger Corman
Directed by Paul Bartel

1975

The Swinging Barmaids
Premiere Releasing
Screenplay by Charles B. Griffith
Produced by Ed Carlin
Directed by Gus Trikonis

(As Director)

1958

Forbidden Island Columbia
Written, Produced and Directed by
Charles B. Griffith

1961

Frontiere Ahead, Hatsankanim
(credits unknown)

Copyright © 1969 Paramount Pictures Corporation

*Roger Vadim directs Jane Fonda in this
scene from Barbarella. Charles Griffith
was one of many writers involved in the
screenplay.*

1976

Eat My Dust New World
Produced by Roger Corman
Written and Directed by
Charles B. Griffith

1979

Up From the Depths New World
Screenplay by Anne Dyer
Produced by Cirio H. Santiago
Directed by Charles B. Griffith

1980

Dr. Heckyl and Mr. Hype Cannon
Produced by Menachem Golan
and Yoram Globus
Written and Directed by
Charles B. Griffith

1981

Smokey Bites the Dust New World
Screenplay by Max Apple
Produced by Roger Corman
Directed by Charles B. Griffith

(As Performer)

1956

It Conquered the World
American International
Screenplay by Lou Rusoff and
(uncredited) Charles B. Griffith
Produced and Directed by
Roger Corman

1957

Attack of the Crab Monsters
Allied Artists
Screenplay by Charles B. Griffith
Produced and Directed by
Roger Corman

The
Musical

ADAPTING POPULAR (OR SOMETIMES obscure) motion pictures to the musical stage is a fairly recent development. For most of theatrical history, the reverse was far more common. Once a show proved its worth on stage, it was scooped up for the movies. *Showboat* and *South Pacific*, for example, began as successful books (by Edna Ferber and James A. Michener, respectively). *Then* they became musicals, then movies. *My Fair Lady* was a straight play (*Pygmalion*, by Shaw) before it was a musical, and then a film. *The Sound of Music* had as its source the real life story of the Baroness Maria Von Trapp and her family of singers, who fled the Nazis during World War II. Only after Rodgers and Hammerstein turned Von Trapp's tale into a hit Broadway show did 20th-Century Fox see fit to make it a movie – the most successful movie musical ever made.

Perhaps because interesting subject matter for musicals is today at a premium, Broadway's tunesmiths have increasingly turned to the big screen for inspiration – often with unexpected and impressive results. Who, for example, would have thought that Federico Fellini's neorealist tale of an Italian prostitute, *Nights of Cabiria* (1957), would be ideal subject matter for a musical? Director-choreographer Bob Fosse did and the show, *Sweet Charity*, was a hit. Needless to say, it then became a movie (with Shirley MacLaine). Likewise Joseph L. Manckiewicz's *All About Eve* (1950), which became *Applause*, starring Lauren Bacall.

And Ingmar Bergman's *Smiles of a Summer Night* (1955), which became *A Little Night Music*. The list, which includes more obvious examples like *Zorba, Singing' in the Rain* and *Smile*, goes on and on.

But Roger Corman's *The Little Shop of Horrors*? An obscure little 1960 B movie about a carnivorous plant? Even Bob Fosse would probably have difficulty seeing that as a subject for a musical, much less one that would, in 1983, win the New York Drama Critics Circle Award, the Drama Desk Award and the Outer Critics' Circle Award as Best Musical of the year, as well as spawn an American touring company, a two-year run in London, and productions in France, Scandinavia, Israel, Japan, Germany, Australia and Iceland.

On the face of it, the idea seems absurd. But actually, the ghoulish *Little Shop* stage show has plenty of antecedents, both here and abroad – going all the way back to Joseph Kesselring's *Arsenic and Old Lace*, Broadway's classic farce about a pair of murderous old women who dispatch victims with poisoned elderberry wine, then dispose of the corpses in the cellar. Though not a musical, *Arsenic*, like *Little Shop*, drew much inspiration from grade B horror movies, particularly those featuring Boris Karloff, who himself played a role in the original Broadway run.

Perhaps a more direct predecessor of *Little Shop*, however, is the Wolf Mankowitz-Monty Norman musical, *Belle or The Ballad of Dr. Crippen*, the story of a man who murders his wife and chops her up in little pieces, which had a successful run in London in 1961. And there was also *The Jack the Ripper Show*, a 1973 London musical about the exploits of Victorian England's most celebrated gaslight ghoul. And, of course, *The Rocky Horror Show*. Not to mention Stephen Sondheim's award-winning *Sweeney Todd*, the tuneful tale of a Victorian butcher who chops his victims up and turns them into meat pies. (*Little Shop* lyricist Howard Asman, in fact, has referred to his show as "Sweeney Pod.") With these as precedents, *Little Shop*'s emergence as a musical seems not just inspired, but almost inevitable.

The Creators

LITTLE SHOP – "THE MUSICAL" IS THE spawn of 39-year-old Howard Ashman, a self-confessed B horror movie addict from Baltimore, who, like so many fans of the Corman cult classic, came upon the film accidentally and never forgot it. A high school student at the time, Ashman caught the film on late night television and began re-imagining it as a theatrical piece even then. It's easy to see why. With its limited sets, humorous dialogue (and *schtick*) and three-act construction, Charles Griffith's screenplay could almost be transferred to the stage as it is. "I thought it was the cleverest, slyest, nastiest thing I'd ever seen in my life," Ashman told *Fangoria* magazine. "You weren't used to seeing send-ups in those days and certainly not as feature films. You might have expected something like that as a sketch on a TV show, but not as a film. So it was unexpected and delicious in its way."

Determined to carve out a theatrical career for himself, Ashman studied theater at Boston University and Indiana University. Over the years, his work as a librettist, lyricist and playwright has been performed at Washington's Arena Stage, Houston Grand Opera, Pittsburgh Light Opera, Princeton's McCarter Theater and Philadelphia's Annenberg Center. He has directed at Arena Stage, Manhattan Theater club, the O'Neill Center's Composer/Librettists Conference and the WPA, a non-profit off-off-Broadway theater where experimental works are showcased for subsequent launch on or off-Broadway. Ashman evenutually became artistic director at the WPA, where *Little Shop of Horrors* was first performed.

Ashman's chief collaborator on the project was composer Alan Menken. The pair met in 1978 at a musical theater workshop operated by the music-licensing organization, BMI (Broadcast Music, Inc.) Ashman was looking for a composer/collaborator and Menken came highly recommended by the man in charge of the workshop, veteran Broadway conductor Lehman Engel – to whom Ashman and Menken would dedicate the original cast recording of their *Little Shop of Horrors.*

Unlike Ashman, Menken had not aimed for a career in the theater. A native of New Rochelle, a suburb of New York City, he went to New York University to study medicine but got hooked on music instead. He performed for a while with his own band, then went on to compose jingles for television commercials. His other work for television includes composing music and lyrics for the daytime soaps *Love of Life* and *Search for Tomorrow*, as well as *Sesame Street*. When he and Howard Ashman met, Menken was studying at Lehman Engel's Musical Theater Workshop at BMI to develop his skills in musical theater.

Ashman and Menken are nothing if not ambitious. Their first collaboration was a musical adaptation of Kurt Vonnegut, Jr.'s satiric 1965 novel, *God Bless You, Mr. Rosewater*, which Ashman read in high school and, like *Little Shop*, began transferring in his mind to the stage even then. Vonnegut's novel, which bears the subtitle *Pearls Before Swine*, recounts the absurdist tale of multi-millionaire Eliot Rosewater, head of a giant philanthropic organization, who dedicates his life to doing good deeds and lavishing concern on assorted low-lifes and unabashedly useless people – a sort of modern variation on Dostoyevsky's *The Idiot*. Ashman wrote the script and lyrics (with additional lyrics supplied by Dennis Green) and Menken composed the score. Like *Little Shop, God Bless You, Mr. Rosewater*

Far out as it may seem, the ghoulish Little Shop *has plenty of theatrical antecedents – dating all the way back to Broadway's classic farce,* Arsenic and Old Lace. *Shown here: Josephine Hull, Jean Adair and Cary Grant in Frank Capra's 1944 movie adaptation of the play.*

Courtesy Jerry Ohlinger's Movie Material Store

was showcased at the WPA Theater, then went on to achieve a successful off-Broadway run. Ashman and Menken were off and running.

Taking his cue from the unexpected success of *Rosewater*—a tale of innocence, fame, media manipulation and greed—Ashman began devising an even more far-out follow-up with similar themes. "I was looking for a project that had something special about it that nobody had done before," he said. "The idea of doing a monster movie for the stage—not a horror movie, but a monster movie for the stage—the idea of doing something about a creature from another world, I don't think anyone's ever done that, certainly not as a musical." And so he began concocting a plot, about a carnivorous plant that brings fame then doom to its nebbish creator, not realizing that he was subconsciously regurgitating the plot of the Corman film he'd seen so long ago. When he caught it again on television, however, he immediately realized where his inspiration had come from, threw out his first draft, and started from scratch with the goal of adapting the Corman film to the stage.

Inspired, Ashman and Menken launched quickly into the project, then Ashman approached his agent to secure her endorsement. He screened a copy of the Corman film for her, but his agent, who had never seen the film before, did not share his enthusiasm, thinking the film not only ridiculous (which it is, but charmingly so), but boring(?). She felt it held little prospect for a musical, but when Ashman and Menken played snippets of their score for her, she quickly saw what they were aiming at and climbed on the bandwagon.

Ancillary rights to the film were secured from Corman himself, though the film was in the public domain as Corman had never copyrighted it. Charles Griffith, who at one time had planned to write a sequel to *Little Shop* himself, was initially excluded from the deal. According to Corman, this was simply a mistake. As he owned the film, he simply sold the musical adaptation rights. Griffith brought suit, however, and soon got his well-earned piece of the action. In fact, when the play became available to regional and repertory theaters, a clause was included in the licensing contract that the following credit had to appear in all posters and publicity for the play immediately following or under Ashman and Menken's names:

Scott Dickstein/Courtesy Cohoes Musical Hall

"Based on the film by Roger Corman, Screenplay by Charles Griffith."

As artistic director of the WPA Theater, Ashman was assured of a showcase for his new baby. The intimate, 99-seat auditorium proved an ideal setting in which to dazzle audiences with the show's multitude of effects. The show premiered at the WPA on May 6, 1982 and ran through June 6, 1982 for a total of 24 performances before moving to off-Broadway. [In the WPA showcase production, Michael Vale played the part of Mushnik, but Hy Anzell assumed the role in the off-Broadway production.] Word of mouth and reviews were so good that Ashman and Menken believed they had a better than 50-50 shot at launching an off-Broadway production *if* they could find backers, so they entered some selected numbers in a BMI-sponsored audition aimed at securing support for promising shows in progress. Record producer David Geffen, Cameron Macintosh and Broadway's Shubert Organization, a powerful support group for shows indicating commercial promise, agreed to finance an off-Broadway production, which premiered at New York's Orpheum Theater (126 Second Avenue at 8th Street) on July 27, 1982, twenty-one years after the debut of Corman's original low-budget quickie. Tickets ranged from $18.95 to $22.95 a seat! Cast and credits were as follows:

The 1961 Wolf Mankowitz-Monty Norman musical, Belle or The Ballad of Dr. Crippen, *the tuneful tale of a man who murders his wife and chops her up into little pieces, foreshadowed* Little Shop *even more.*

John Clayton/Courtesy *Fangoria* Magazine

Puppeteer Martin P. Robinson manipulates the giant shark's head of Audrey II.

WPA Theater, David Geffen, Cameron Macintosh and the Shubert Organization present a musical in two acts based on a film of the same name by Roger Corman, originally presented by the WPA Theater (Kyle Renick, producing director), with book and lyrics by Howard Ashman; music by Alan Menken. Staged by Howard Ashman. Musical staging, Edie Cowan; scenery, Edward T. Gianfrancesco; lighting, Craig Evans; costumes, Sally Lesser; sound, Otts Munderloh; puppets, Martin P. Robinson; vocal arrangements, musical supervision and musical direction, Robert Billig; orchestrations, Robby Merkin; general manager, Albert Poland; stage manager, Paul Mills Holmes; publicity, Solters & Roskin, Millie Schoenbaum

The Cast*

Chiffon .... Marlene Danielle
Crystal .... Jennifer Leigh Warren
Ronnette .... Sheila Kay Davis
Mushnik .... Hy Anzell
Audrey .... Ellen Greene
Seymour .... Lee Wilkof
Derelict .... Martin P. Robinson
Orin Scrivello, Mr. Bernstein,
Skip Snip, Patrick Martin,
Mrs. Luce and everyone else .... Franc Luz
Audrey II (Manipulation) .... Martin P. Robinson
            (Voice) .... Ron Taylor

*Players who succeeded the original performers in the ensuing years include: Leilani Jones (Chiffon); Fyvush Finkel (Mushnik); Faith Prince, Katherine Meloche (Audrey); Brad Moranz (Seymour); Anthony B. Asbury (Derelict); Robert Frish (Orin, et. al.).

Reviews were not only enthusiastic, but exceptional. The influential *New York Times*, which, although its reviewers deny this, has the power to make or break a show with its notices, wrote: "It leaves the audience feeling just like Audrey II between victims—ravenous for more." *The New Yorker* hailed it as "... a musical comedy that is both musical and comic ... full of surprises and marvelous effects." Said *Business Week*: "... it's charmingly silly and tuneful, with the most ingenious puppetry this side of Miss Piggy." About Audrey II, *Time* magazine wrote: "... a carnivore with its own intimidating charm ... envelops the stage and (gasp!) most of the audience."

Ashman and Menken had a hit on their hands.

Composer Alan Menken (left) and writer-director-lyricist Howard Ashman.

Courtesy Judi Davidson Publicity

Also from the Los Angeles production. Seymour (Lee Wilkof) contemplates doing away with sadistic dentist Orin Scrivello (Franc Luz), who wears a space age gas mask to heighten the pleasure as he dispenses pain.

The Story

PEOPLE FAMILIAR WITH THE CORMAN film are often surprised by how much of it Howard Ashman's stage adaptation actually retains. The musical reflects a genuine fondness for the original and is neither a put down nor a send-up—the latter would have been very difficult indeed considering the fact that the original itself was a send-up. Like the original, the play is a satire of B science-fiction movies with a lot of tongue-in-cheek humor. But Ashman does not make fun of the characters or their desperate situation. Quite the contrary. By emphasizing the Faustian sub-theme Griffith had loosely sketched into this script, Ashman's adaptation takes on

a more serious and emotional tone. In the original, the plant, though just as vocal, brings fame and fortune to the shop merely because of its existence. In the musical, however, the plant becomes a genuine character, a seductive Mephistophelian weed that pointedly spells out the riches it can bring to Seymour. [But then, in the play, the plant has a larger game plan as it is out to conquer the world (like some kind of Triffid), an implication only hinted at in the original film.]

Ashman does reduce the cast of offbeat characters, however. Considerably, in fact. Gone from the stage adaptation are the memorable Mrs. Krelboined, the flower-eating Burson Fouch, the dilettante Mrs. Fishtwanger, detectives Joe Fink and Frank Stoolie, the seductive Leonora Clyde and the always-in-mourning Mrs. Shiva [though the dialogue does refer to this character several times as being the shop's best funeral customer]. Ashman expands the role of Griffith's pain-dispensing dentist, Dr. Phoebus Farb, but changes his name to Orin Scrivello. Curiously though, he eliminates the dentist's most memorable victim, the masochistic Wilbur Force, a character reinserted in the subsequent movie version of the musical.

Gone too are Seymour's teenaged groupies from the local high school who seek to feature Audrey Jr. in their high school parade. In their place, Ashman substitutes three black female street urchins with the sixties rock 'n' roll-ish names of Crystal, Ronnette and Chiffon, who not only take part in the play's action, but comment on it as well, functioning as a sort of Greek Chorus.

Ashman sets the action in the sixties, the period of the original film, and retains the skid row setting— though he transposes it from Los Angeles to New York's East Side.

Most of the action takes place inside Mushnik's Flower Shop, a dump of a place going fast to ruin due to lack of customers, run by the irascible Mr. Mushnik. The shop has two employees: Seymour *Krelborn* (whom Mushnik plucked from an orphanage to work for him), the archetypal nerd, and Audrey, a voluptuous but sweet bleached blonde whom Seymour secretly loves from afar. Ashman eliminates Audrey's penchant for malapropisms, but adds a depth to her character not present in the original film. A waif with little self-esteem (much like Seymour himself), Audrey subjects herself to constant verbal as well as physical abuse from her affluent boyfriend, sadistic dentist Orin Scrivello, who, striking an Elvis Presley pose, wears a black leather jacket and rides a motorcycle whenever he comes to call.

In the manner of a fifties science-fiction movie, the show opens as an ominous off-stage voice (Franc Luz) sets the scene by warning the audience of a terrifying threat to earthly existence that appeared one day not too long ago " ... in the most innocent and unlikely of places." The plot then revolves around nebbish Seymour's nurturing of a bizarre plant, a sort of flytrap, that he got from a mysterious Oriental from whom he occasionally buys cuttings to conduct his botanical experiments. He keeps the baby plant in a flower pot.

The skid row florist shop where Seymour works is on the verge of bankruptcy and its owner, Mr. Mushnik, is desperate. There's no longer any money to pay Seymour or his other employee, Audrey, with whom Seymour is secretly in love. He has even named the plant after her, calling it Audrey II. Seymour shows the weird plant (which made humming noises during a recent eclipse) to Mushnik, but the man is unimpressed. Alone with Audrey II, Seymour sings to it ("Grow For Me") and the plant's tiny jaws open wide. When Seymour cuts his finger on one of the plant's spikey thorns and Audrey II hungrily scarfs down the drops of blood, he reacts in horror. But when he sees that his blood has caused the plant to grow twice its size in twenty-four hours, he realizes he's on to something and pricks his remaining fingers so that the plant will flourish even more.

Notoriety descends upon Seymour as Audrey II grows bigger. Business at the shop starts to boom. Mushnik is so delighted that he decides to adopt Seymour and call the shop "Mushnik and Son." But then the plant starts to wilt and die. It needs more food, but Seymour, who has begun to look a little anemic to everyone, is bone dry. In one of the show's funniest numbers, Audrey II, in a booming voice, presents Seymour with the Faustian solution. In exchange for a whopping big meal, Audrey II guarantees Seymour fame and fortune ("A Cadillac car and a guest shot on Jack Paar.") The ideal victim soon presents himself in the form of Orin Scrivello, Audrey's bullying boyfriend. Seymour pays a visit to the dentist, ostensibly to have

his teeth looked at, but actually to slay him with a knife. But he can't go through with the murder. To increase the pleasure he will get from inflicting pain on his new patient, Scrivello dons a special gas mask that looks like a space helmet. But the helmet locks and he's accidentally asphyxiated. Seymour chops the body up in little pieces, takes it back to the shop, and feeds it to the grateful plant, which proceeds to grow even bigger.

As Audrey II promised, fame and fortune rain upon Seymour. TV talk shows seek him out. The William Morris Agency is determined to sign him up. But, most importantly, Audrey, now free of the victimizing Scrivello, has fallen in love with Seymour and she dreams of getting married and settling down "Somewhere That's Green."

But Audrey II's appetite has barely been whetted. The plant demands more food. Mushnik finds out what's been happening and Seymour has little choice but to feed his new-found "Dad" to the insatiable weed. Overcome with guilt, Seymour decides to supply no more bodies, so the plant turns on its namesake. Seymour manages to pull Audrey out of the plant's jaws in time, but she is mortally wounded. In a spirit of self-sacrifice, Audrey tells Seymour to feed her to the plant when she dies so that it will continue to bring him the riches he needs. Then she expires in his arms. Grief-stricken, Seymour feeds her to the plant. But wealth and fame prove to be hollow without her and Seymour decides to kill the plant. He tries

The irascible Mushnik (Hy Anzell), whose shop is on the verge of bankruptcy, dismisses Seymour's (Lee Wilkof) bizarre new plant as too little and too late.

Peter Cunningham

to poison it, but the plant spits the poison out. Brandishing a machete, Seymour dives inside the plant to chop it up from inside. But Audrey II devours him instead and spits out the machete.

By this time, Audrey II has grown so large that it takes up most of the shop as well as the stage. It blooms and in its petals appear the faces of its victims: Scrivello, Mushnik, Audrey and Seymour who admonish the audience not to feed any plant it may come across that looks like Audrey II. Crystal, Ronnette and Chiffon re-appear to join in the warning chant, but Audrey II has the last word. Its monstrous jaws open wide and its vines spring into the audience. Simultaneously, more tendrils drop on the spectators from the theater ceiling and the stage goes black as the carnivorous plant's jaws snap victoriously shut.

The Performers

WRITER-DIRECTOR ASHMAN'S *LITTLE Shop of Horrors* is marvelous fun and an extremely inventive theatrical experience. [We'll get to its ingenious special effects shortly.] But some critics have pointed out that the score itself boasts few numbers destined for musical theater immortality. It's true that few of Ashman/Menken's songs stand very well on their own ("Somewhere That's Green" is, perhaps, the one exception). But so what? Individually and collectively, the show's 16 numbers are so amusing, tuneful and perfectly tied to both story

Little Shop's Tunes and Who Sings 'Em

ACT I

"Prologue (Little Shop of Horrors)" : Chiffon, Crystal and Ronnette

"Skid Row (Downtown)" : Entire Company

"Da-Doo" : Chiffon, Crystal and Ronnette

"Grow For Me" : Seymour

"Don't It Go To Show Ya Never Know"
Mushnik, Seymour, Chiffon, Crystal and Ronnette

"Somewhere That's Green" : Audrey

"Closed for Renovations" : Seymour, Audrey and Mushnik

"Dentist!" : Orin, Chiffon, Crystal and Ronnette

"Mushnik and Son" : Mushnik and Seymour

"Feed Me (Git It)" : Seymour and Audrey II

"Now (It's Just the Gas)" : Orin and Seymour

ACT II

"Call Back in the Morning" : Seymour and Audrey

"Suddenly, Seymour" : Seymour and Audrey

"Suppertime" : Audrey II

"The Meek Shall Inherit" : Entire Company

"Finale (Don't Feed the Plants)" : Entire Company

and character that to criticize them for having little "Top 40" potential seems like carping.

"Somewhere That's Green" is a good example. In it, the put-upon Audrey sings yearningly of what life in the suburbs, away from skid row, would be like with Seymour. Her romantic vision is drawn almost exclusively from television. "I'm his December Bride," she sings. "He's Father, he Knows Best. Our kids watch Howdy Doody. As the sun sets in the west." The song is bitingly satiric, yes, but it is also quite touching —almost a ballad—especially as sung by Ellen Greene, who does a marvelous impression of Judy Holliday's Billie Dawn character [from *Born Yesterday*] in the number. Her Audrey, in fact, is a comic amalgam of Judy Holliday and Marilyn Monroe, combining the former's deceptive dumbness with the latter's breathy innocence. Greene says the character first came into focus for her during costume fittings for the show. "We went through about five wigs before Audrey became a cornsilk blonde. Next came the low-cut leotard skin dresses, stiletto heels and jangling earrings of the B-movie heroines who are Audrey's role models."

Courtesy Judi Davidson Publicity

Lee Wilkof and Ellen Greene recreate their roles as the star-crossed lovers, Seymour and Audrey, for the Los Angeles production of the hit Ashman/Menken musical.

Greene has since turned the character of Audrey very much into her own, having played the role not only off-Broadway, but in the Los Angeles and London productions, as well as the subsequent movie version.

Ellen Greene, who heralds from New York City, made her Broadway debut in the short-lived musical *Rachel Lily Rosenblum And Don't You Forget It* by Paul Jabara and Tom Eyen. The show, which was produced by Robert Stigwood, premiered at the Broadhurst Theater on November 26, 1973 and closed December 1. It was followed by other roles, on and off-Broadway, in *In the Boom Boom Room* (by David Rabe); a revival of *The Threepenny Opera*; *The Nature and Purpose of the Universe*; *Teeth 'n' Smiles*; *The Sorrows of Stephen*; *Disrobing the Bride*; and *The Little Prince and the Aviator*. Prior to her starring role in the film version of *Little Shop of Horrors*, she made a flashy appearance in film director Paul Mazursky's comic theatrical memoir, *Next Stop, Greenwich Village* (1976), opposite Christopher Walken and Shelley Winters, where she was singled out by critic Pauline Kael. Kael has termed her, " ... a weird little wow," and continues: "When she lifts from her mousey little-Audrey manner of speech to her big Broadway singing voice (it's like pent-up passion being released), you're even more transfixed —you don't know where that sound can be coming from." *Time* magazine called her Audrey: " ... a sweet, sexy, slightly dizzy blonde with an Elmer Fudd lisp, 'wittle-girl' wiles and a voice that buckles theater walls."

Apart from Ashman and Menken, Ellen Greene, the only member of the original off-Broadway cast to recreate her role on screen, seems to have gained the most from her connection with *Little Shop*. Her stage and screen career, especially since the film, is definitely on the rise. But the

debut in *Present Tense*, then landed the role of Seymour in *Little Shop*.

Hy Anzell, an off-Broadway veteran, makes an ideally combustible Mushnik, a character who, according to writer Ashman, "seldom smiles but often sweats." The musical *Little Shop*

Scott Dickstein/Courtesy Cohoes Musical Hall

show's other main leads received excellent notices as well, particularly Lee Wilkof as the nerdish but well meaning Seymour, whose voice at times is startlingly (intentionally?) reminiscent of Jonathan Haze. A graduate of the University of Cincinnati, Wilkof made his off-Broadway

Now available to regional, summer and community theaters all across the country, Little Shop of Horrors *is proving a hit from coast to coast. Here, Patrick Richwood as Seymour struggles to maintain his composure as Audrey II promises him riches beyond his wildest imaginings in the song "Git It!." From the Cohoes Musical Hall (Troy, New York) production.*

does tend to downplay the ethnic Jewish humor that ran through the original film, however. In particular, Anzell's accent (unlike Mel Welles') is less Eastern European than middle class New York.

Finally, there is the ubiquitous Franc Luz, who not only plays the Elvis Presley-imitating dentist, Orin Scrivello, but a slew of other parts as well. Including: a wino who appears in the show's opening scene; a customer in the shop; a radio announcer; Mrs. Luce, the unctuous wife of an unnamed publishing magnate who wants to put Seymour's puss on the cover of *Life*; Mr. Bernstein, a loud-mouthed NBC producer who wants Seymour to star in a series called "Gardening Tips"; Patrick Martin, a sleazeball merchandiser for World Botanical Enterprises, who wants to make cuttings from Audrey II and shop them all over the world; and William Morris agent Skip Snip ("It's nice to meet me, the pleasure is yours."), who wants to sign Seymour up as a client. [Perhaps for cost or cast-saving reasons, the actor who plays Scrivello also plays all these same parts in regional or repertory productions of the play as well.] Born in Cambridge, Massachusetts, Luz, a graduate of New Mexico State University, made his off-Broadway debut in a 1974 revival of Richard Brinsley Sheridan's *The Rivals*. This was followed by another off-Broadway revival of the popular musical *Fiorello!* In 1979, he appeared in the Broadway production of *Whoopee!* then moved on to *Little Shop*.

As good as all these performers are, the real star of the show, of course, is the garrulous, people-eating plant, Audrey II.

The Special Effects

THE GREATEST CHALLENGE HOWARD Ashman faced in bringing *Little Shop of Horrors* to the stage was the character of Audrey II. The plot hinges on the leafy carnivore, which, during the course of the show's two acts, grows from a potted pipsqueak less than a foot in height to a fabulous fly-trap—with shark-like mouth and teeth —that all but fills up the entire stage. To mesh with the musical's broad theatricality, Audrey II couldn't just be a lump. Audiences had to *believe* in it—in all its incarnations—for the show to work. It had to be made as real a character as Seymour, Audrey, Mushnik and all the others. A character that could sing, sway to the music, do double takes, and, finally, gobble up the cast. But how to do it?

Ashman was convinced that the effect he wanted could be pulled off —not easily, perhaps, but believably —with the use of hand puppets. The art of puppetry had made tremendous strides over the years. Jim Hensen's Muppet characters, for example, had virtually became cultural heroes, as believable to audiences in their exaggerated way as the characters on your average television sitcom. Pulling off such tricks on television and in the movies, where all the paraphernalia needed to manipulate the puppets could be easily concealed out of frame, was one thing, however. It would be quite another to deliver the same goods on stage, where Audrey II is in full view of the audience at all times.

Ashman approached a number of well-known puppeteers to help him out, but was turned down. One of them, however, recommended an up-and-coming actor/puppeteer named Martin P. Robinson, who had worked with Hensen's Muppets on *Sesame Street* (Robinson appeared on the show as Mr. Snuffleupgaus), as well as Bill Baird's Marionettes. A horror movie fan who numbered Corman's off-the-wall classic as one of his favorites, Robinson eagerly accepted the challenge of bringing Audrey II to life on stage.

The plant's initial appearance presented little difficulty, Robinson says. It debuts in a flower pot placed on a window seat where all it has to do is snap open its tiny mouth hungrily when Seymour cuts his finger on one of the plant's thorns and drips blood for the first time. Robinson, concealed beneath the window seat, achieved the effect by pulling on a pair of strings attached to the plant's movable jaws. *Presto!* The mouth opened and closed. Other strings were attached to the plant's leaves so that, with a slight tug, Robinson could cause them to wilt on cue.

Ron Taylor – the voice of Audrey II.

Following its gluttonous orgy, Audrey II doubles in size and Seymour appears on stage with it cradled in his left arm to show it off proudly to the street urchins and Mushnik. As the street urchins launch into song, the plant sways to the music, then grows bored and literally tries to bite the hand that feeds him—in fact, *eat* it! Robinson achieved this remarkable effect again quite simply. The puppet is actually being manipulated by Seymour himself, whose real left arm is inside the puppet, whereas the arm that's cradling the puppet is a fake.

By the end of the first act, Audrey II has tripled in size and become quite vocal. Ron Taylor's deep voice off-stage—to which the plant's mouth and body movements were perfectly timed —added yet another dimension of believability to the character. Even the plant's roots come alive at this point, spilling out over the rim of the pot the plant is encased in and dancing in step to the music. Robinson achieved this effect by merging puppet and puppeteer into one. From inside, he manipulated the pod with his own torso and arms while his legs, stuck inside the thick roots, enabled the roots to flail about.

For the plant's fourth and final metamorphosis where it all but covers the stage, Robinson, again from inside the puppet, manipulated the body and roots as before, but by this time, the plant's branches have also gotten into the act as they reach out and grab people. This was achieved with the help of the stage crew who manipulated the branches.

Lee Wilkof, Ellen Greene and Hy Anzell.

Peter Cunningham

Robinson brought off the finale —where the plant's leaves blossom to reveal the singing faces of its four victims—by making rubber life masks of the principals involved. As the performers crooned off stage, the stage crew manipulated the lifelike masks by hand in perfect sync to their vocalizations. [In some productions, these vocalizations are put on tape for even greater control.] The effect is quite magical.

Other effects such as the plant's gobbling up victims were achieved by having the actor-victims climb into the pod, then disappear through a special slit. Audrey II's spitting out of unwanted foodstuffs was achieved by having a hidden member of the stage crew toss the item from the plant's mouth. In one of the more ghoulish odes to the original film, Seymour also stuffs pieces of the late but unlamented dentist's body into the plant's jaws, including a pile of intestines, which the rapturous carnivore gobbles up like spaghetti.

When the off-Broadway production of *Little Shop of Horrors* proved to be a runaway hit, there was immediate talk of moving the show to one of Broadway's larger theaters. The show's creators demurred, however, appealing as that prospect was. For they firmly believed that another compelling reason for the show's effectiveness, particularly in the area of special effects, was the size of the

In a spirit of self-sacrifice, the mortally wounded Audrey (Ellen Greene) tells Seymour (Lee Wilkof) to feed her to the plant when she dies so that it will continue to bring him the riches he deserves.

theater itself.

"*Little Shop* works best in a small theater, not a large auditorium," Ashman says. "The plant is a fixed size, just as people are. If you look at our plant that looks so enormous and funny and a little scary at the end, it's 18 feet long in a 25-foot proscenium. In a 50-foot proscenium, 18 feet is *not* very big." And so the show remained at the intimate Orpheum Theater, where it played for several years."

3

The Movie Musical

The Flowering of "Little Shop"

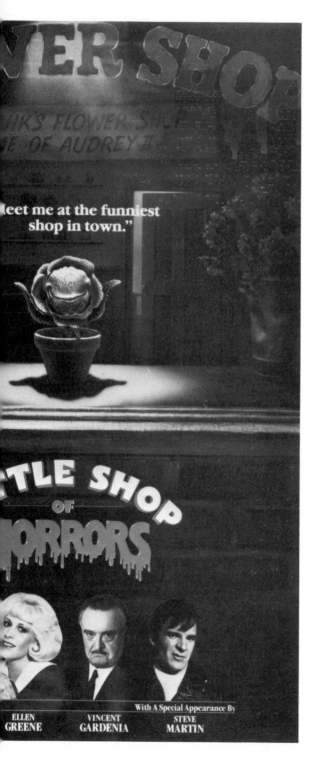

AT THE SHOW'S ROUSING CONCLU-sion, the street urchins sing prophetically of the fate of Audrey II and its malignant spawn. The plants spread their influence from coast to coast, then all over the world. This fate was reflected in real life. Less than a year after the play debuted at the Orpheum Theater, it moved to Los Angeles, opening at the Westwood Playhouse on April 27 with Ellen Greene, Lee Wilkof, Franc Luz and Martin P. Robinson recreating the roles they originated off-Broadway. Then the show moved to London. It has since become available to regional, community and summer theaters all across the country—such as the Cohoes Music Hall in Troy, New York, where it was a sell-out for its six-week run in late 1986. Some theaters even share props and special effects ideas with each other.

Ashman and Menken's *Little Shop of Horrors* gives every sign of becoming a cult favorite like *Arsenic and Old Lace*, which remains the most frequently performed comedy of murders in American theater history.

Needless to say, the success of Ashman and Menken's potted brain-child was something of which Hollywood could not fail to take notice. As early as 1983, rumors of a planned movie version of the show began to circulate in the trades. Not until 1985, however, did the following notice appear in *Variety*:

WB Buys Whole 'Shop'

Little Shop of Horrors, the legit tuner spoof of sci-fi films based on the 1958 [sic] Roger Corman film of the same name, has been sold to Warner Brothers for $500,000, to be produced in partnership with David Geffen, one of the producers of the stage version. As has been rumored, Steven Spielberg will produce and Martin Scorsese will direct, with Howard Ashman scripting from his original stage book and Alan Menken repeating as composer. Plan is to transfer the tuner as is, with exception of all the music. Ashman said some of the existing tunes will be dropped and the duo will be writing more.

Alas, even the show biz bible could be wrong! For by the time *Little Shop of Horrors* did reach the screen, almost a year later, Spielberg and Scorsese would be gone [as would some of the songs; in this the article proved correct], replaced at the helm by David Geffen and by Frank Oz, one of the original creators of the Muppets.

The Reviews

LITTLE SHOP OF HORRORS *IS A FRACtured, funny production transported rather reluctantly from the stage to the screen. Kooky songs about a boy, a girl and a man-eating plant may have been swell entertainment in the theater, but come up a bit soft in the cinema. Nonetheless, production is offbeat enough to win a cult audience and perhaps a bit of crossover from the mainstream ... Individually,* Little Shop of Horrors *is filled with many memorable moments. It is the cumulative effect that is rather slight.*
— *Variety* **(December 10, 1986)**

Little Shop of Horrors *comes off well ... Rick Moranis, as the wide-eyed simpleton; Ellen Greene, as the paintpot princess of his heart; Vincent Gardenia, as the fretful owner of the shop, all do their caricaturing well enough. Steve Martin, as Greene's boyfriend—a sadistic dentist—does his frenetic best to shuck his amateurish self-consciousness, and nearly succeeds. The songs by Alan Menken and Howard Ashman leak past, inoffensively.* — *The New Republic* **(January 26, 1987)**

Little Shop of Horrors *is jivey, senseless fun. The stupidity is appealing, the way it is in great comic strips. These moviemakers aren't trying to edify us or make us see beauty in the skid-row settings—they're just out to make us feel brainlessly slaphappy gaga ...* — *The New Yorker* **(January 12, 1987)**

Given the lumbering material, Frank Oz's film of Little Shop of Horrors is surprisingly light on its feet. It doesn't overflow and carry you off, the way a big-budget musical ought to—even with the bloodletting, it's anemic. But Oz does clean work ... The performance that busts the movie open ... is Steve Martin's turn as Audrey's sadistic-biker-dentist boyfriend. If nothing else, it's one of the best interpretations of Elvis Presley ever ... When Martin leaves the picture, there are no more wild cards ... This Little Shop isn't Corman's Little Shop— its integrity belongs to the world of Broadway musicals, not low-budget black comedies. The finish with guts would have ended this shindig on a sour note. It would have been like watching Miss Piggy get roasted on a spit. — *Village Voice* **(December 23, 1986)**

Seymour (Rick Moranis) pleads with Audrey II to grow. Which it does. And does. And does.

A Geffen Company Presentation of a Frank Oz Film.

The Cast

Seymour Krelborn	RICK MORANIS
Audrey	ELLEN GREENE
Mushnik	VINCENT GARDENIA
Orin Scrivello, D.D.S.	STEVE MARTIN
Crystal	TICHINA ARNOLD
Chiffon	TISHA CAMPBELL
Ronnette	MICHELLE WEEKS
Patrick Martin	JAMES BELUSHI
Wink Wilkinson	JOHN CANDY
First Customer	CHRISTOPHER GUEST
Arthur Denton	BILL MURRAY
Narrator	STANLEY JONES
"Downtown" Old Woman	BEATRICE READING
"Downtown" Bum #1	ED WILEY
"Downtown" Bum #2	ALAN TILVERN
"Downtown" Bum #3	JOHN SCOTT MARTIN
Chinese Florist	VINCENT WONG
Doo Wop Street Singers	MAK WILSON, DANNY CUNNINGHAM, DANNY JOHN-JULES, GARY PALMER, PAUL SWABY
Second Customer	MILDRED SHAY
Third Customer	MELISSA WILTSIE
Fourth Customer	KEVIN SCOTT
Fifth Customer	BARBARA ROSENBLAT
Radio Station Assistant	ADEEN FOGLE
Audrey & Seymour's Kids	KELLY HUNTLEY, PAUL REYNOLDS
Dental Nurse	MIRIAM MARGOLYES
Boy Patient	ABBIE DABNER
Second Patient	FRANK DUX
Patient on Ceiling	PETER WHITMAN
Girl Patient	HEATHER HENSON
Girl's Mother	JUDITH MORSE
Agent	BOB SHERMAN
"Life" Magazine Lady	DOREEN HERMITAGE
Her Assistant	KERRY SHALE
Network Executive #1	ROBERT ARDEN
Network Executive #2	STEPHEN HOYE
Network Executive #3	BOB SESSIONS
Television Reporter	MICHAEL J. SHANNON
The Voice of Audrey II	LEVI STUBBS (of The Four Tops)

The Credits

Director	FRANK OZ
Producer	DAVID GEFFEN
Screenplay	HOWARD ASHMAN
Audrey II Designed and Created by	LYLE CONWAY
Choreography	PAT GARRETT
Film Editor	JOHN JYMPSON
Director of Photography	ROBERT PAYNTER, B.S.C.
Production Designer	ROY WALKER
Special Visual Effects	BRAN FERREN
Music Produced by	BOB GAUDIO
Original Motion Picture Score	MILES GOODMAN
Line Producer	WILLIAM S. GILMORE
Music	ALAN MENKEN
Lyrics	HOWARD ASHMAN
Associate Producers	DAVID ORTON AND DENIS HOLT

Filmed at Pinewood Studios Ltd.,
Iver Heath, Buckinghamshire, England

Color by Technicolor

Distributed by Warner Bros.
(A Warner Communications Company)

Running Time: 88 Minutes

MPAA Rating: PG–13

The plant itself is a marvelous creation —a cross between Pac Man and Jaws —that, whenever it flips its petals, emits a funky and resonant baritone. The score is consistently witty, and the various roles have been sharply cast... Best of all though is Steve Martin, whose rendition of a sadistic dentist-soon-to-be-plant-food is sheer comic genius and whose musical number, 'Be a Dentist,' is such an instant side-splitting classic that it goes a long way toward making Little Shop of Horrors *an instant comedy classic itself.*
— **Glamour (February, 1987)**

The Little Shop of Horrors *is a new film based on an off-Broadway musical based on an earlier film by Roger*

Corman, master of the schlock, low-budget, horror movie. It has trekked the route from grotesquerie through tunefulness to jolly absurdity without ever passing by good taste. Nevertheless, what it lacks (or completely violates) in manners, it sometimes compensates for in refreshingly bizarre humor... But often the film simply disgusts... [and] when Audrey II acquires the recognizably black voice of Levi Stubbs (one of The Four Tops) late in the film, it is not just dramatically ineffective, but racially bothersome. — **Commonweal (January 30, 1987)**

You can try not liking this adaptation of the off-Broadway musical hit—it has no polish and a pushy way with a gag—but the movie sneaks up on you, about as subtly as Audrey II. The songs are neat pastiches of '60s pop.

Audrey (Ellen Greene) fantasizes about life in the suburbs, far away from skid row, with the song "Somewhere That's Green."

The tuneful street urchins (Tichina Arnold, Tisha Campbell and Michelle Weeks) strut their stuff. Production designer Roy Walker's impressive and very realistic skid row set was built entirely on the "007 Stage" at Pinewood Studios in England.

The plant is an animatronic wonder, all blue gums, naughty tendrils and mighty mouth. Moranis and Greene make for a comely-homely pair of thwarted lovers, and Martin is his hilarious self, libeling all dentists who had just managed to forget Marathon Man* **— *Time* magazine (December 29, 1986)**

* *Time*'s reviewer wasn't far off. Shortly after the film's release, a story in the Los Angeles *Herald-Examiner* reported that as a result of Martin's on-screen antics, a Beverly Hills dentist named Roger Lewis had decided to launch a public protest about the film. "While I found the scene in *Little Shop* hysterically funny, I couldn't help but wonder ... just how much this brief bellylaugh was costing my profession," Lewis was quoted as saying. According to the article, Lewis challenged Martin to do some public service spots on behalf of the dental industry in order to counter the negative publicity. As an incentive, Lewis added, "I will personally provide him [Martin] with free dental care, and all of my colleagues will sign a written statement *never* to try to get into the acting profession." The outcome of this *cause célèbre* is unknown.

The Performers

RICK MORANIS
as Seymour

THE TORONTO-BORN MORANIS BEGAN his showbiz career as a part time technician for a local radio station while he was still in high school. He began writing one-liners for the deejays on the station and his jokes proved so inventive and funny that he was eventually given his own show,

Seymour (Rick Moranis) and Audrey (Ellen Greene) discover they're falling in love.

becoming a popular on-air personality while still in his teens. Settling firmly on a showbiz career, he began performing stand-up routines in local cabarets and nightclubs, then landed some spots on Canadian television. After several years of writing and performing on Canadian TV, he came to the attention of the producers of the satiric and very popular *Second City Television* show, then in its third year. A big hit in Canada, *SCTV* was also syndicated in America, where Moranis won Emmys in 1981 and

The citizens of skid row sing longingly for escape from their dismal surroundings in the opening number "Downtown."

1982 for his writing on the show. Moranis and *SCTV* cohort Dave Thomas created the popular McKenzie Brothers—two beer-swilling philosophers from the Canadian north woods named Bob and Doug, whose goofy, slobbering antics became one of the most popular features of the show. The pair created a McKenzie Brothers comedy album, which went on to win a Grammy nomination, then a McKenzie Brothers film, *Strange Brew* (1983), which the pair co-wrote, co-directed and co-starred in. Max Von Sydow, of all people, was also featured in the cast—along with the voice of Mel Blanc! The following year, Moranis appeared in Walter Hill's rock 'n' roll *film noir Streets of Fire*, and in 1986 co-starred with Robin Williams and Peter O'Toole in *Club Paradise*, directed by fellow *SCTV* alumnus Harold Ramis [*SCTV*ers Eugene Levy, Andrea Martin, and Joe Flaherty also had bits in the film]. However, it was Moranis' co-starring role in the blockbuster comedy *Ghostbusters* (1984) as Sigourney Weaver's endlessly partying neighbor that brought him to the attention of the producers of *Little Shop* and earned him the role of Seymour. He has since appeared in Mel Brooks' *Star Wars* send-up, *Spaceballs* (1987), where he plays the inept villain "Dark Helmet."

ELLEN GREENE
as Audrey

A NATIVE NEW YORKER, WHOSE grandfather was in Yiddish theater,

Greene created the role of Audrey off-Broadway, playing the role for two years—18 months in New York and Los Angeles and six months in London's West End. Although her father was a dentist and her two brothers were, respectively, a doctor and a lawyer, her education-oriented family didn't stand in her way when she started calling on casting agents after finishing high school. She began her career as a cabaret singer, then began landing roles off-Broadway [see Part II]. She made her film debut in Paul Mazursky's *Next Stop, Greenwich Village* (1976), then played opposite Jill Clayburgh in *I'm Dancing As Fast As I Can* in 1982.

VINCENT GARDENIA
as Mushnik

GARDENIA WAS BORN IN NAPLES, Italy in 1922. He played his first role at the age of five—in Brooklyn, where his family settled after emigrating to the U.S. Graduating from juvenile to leading roles in New York's Italian theater, Gardenia came to the attention of Broadway and Hollywood in an off-Broadway adaptation of Nelson Algren's novel about drug addiction, *Man With The Golden Arm* (1954). The novel was filmed the following year by Otto Preminger (starring Frank Sinatra, who earned himself an Oscar nomination). Gardenia appeared on and off- Broadway in productions of *The Brothers Karamazov, The Visit, Death of a Salesman* and *A View From the Bridge*, then won a Tony for his performance in Neil

Simon's *The Prisoner of Second Avenue*. He has since appeared in three other Simon plays: *God's Favorite*, *Plaza Suite* and *California Suite*, as well as David Mamet's *Glengarry Glen Ross*. His movies include *Murder Inc.* (1960), *Death Wish* (1974), Billy Wilder's *The Front Page* (1974) and Warren Beatty's *Heaven Can Wait* (1978). Gardenia earned a Best Supporting Actor nomination in 1973 for his characteristically irascible performance as the manager of a baseball team in *Bang The Drum Slowly* [he lost to John Houseman for *The Paper Chase*].

STEVE MARTIN
as Orin Scrivello

MARTIN, EVERYBODY'S FAVORITE "wild and crazy guy," was born in Waco, Texas but raised in Southern California. He got his first taste of show business selling guidebooks at Disneyland in Anaheim. Hooked on magic and comedy, he began performing tricks and schticks while in his teens. He later attended UCLA, earning a degree in theater arts. At 21, he landed a spot as a comedy writer on *The Smothers Brothers Comedy Hour* and won an Emmy. In the late sixties, he began performing his own stand-up comedy routines in concert, serving as the opening act for such music groups as The Car-

Mushnik (Vincent Gardenia) threatens to expose Seymour (Rick Moranis) when he discovers the reason for the plant's unbelievable growth. Seymour's problem is momentarily solved when his employer becomes the plant's next snack.

Audrey (Ellen Greene), Mushnik (Vincent Gardenia) and Seymour (Rick Moranis) celebrate the fact that Audrey II has wrought a financial bonanza.

penters and The Nitty Gritty Dirt Band. Subsequent appearances on *The Tonight Show* (with Johnny Carson) catapulted him to fame. He has won Grammys for his comedy albums (*Let's Get Small* and *A Wild and Crazy Guy*) and got a 1978 Oscar nomination in the short film category for his clever film *The Absent-Minded Waiter*. His feature films include Carl Reiner's *The Jerk* (1979), *Dead Men Don't Wear Plaid*

JAMES BELUSHI
as Patrick Martin

BROTHER OF THE LATE JOHN BELUSHI, James Belushi was born and raised

Seymour (Rick Moranis) gets his first look at Audrey's (Ellen Greene) abusive "boyfriend," sadistic dentist and Elvis clone, Orin Scrivello (Steve Martin).

(1982), *The Man With Two Brains* (1983) and *All of Me* (1984), as well as Harold Ross' serio-comic musical *Pennies From Heaven* (1981) and John Landis' *Three Amigos* (1986). Following his show-stopping appearance in *Little Shop*, Martin starred in an updated comedy version of "Cyrano De Bergerac" called *Roxanne* (1987), which he also scripted, and with John Candy in the "road" comedy, *Planes, Trains and Automobiles* (1987).

in Chicago. A graduate of the University of Illinois, he earned his comic spurs performing for two years with Chicago's famed *Second City* troupe before moving to New York. There he appeared in Joseph Papp's revival of the Gilbert and Sullivan opera *The Pirates of Penzance* as well as NBC's *Saturday Night Live*. He made his film debut opposite James Caan in Michael Mann's crime drama *Thief* (1982) then turned to comedy in *Trading Places* (1983) opposite Eddie Murphy and *The Man With One Red Shoe* (1985). He earned an Oscar nomination as Best Supporting Actor as James Woods' doper compatriot in Oliver Stone's *Salvador.*

James Belushi as high-powered hustler Patrick Martin, who hopes to get rich by selling "cuttings" from Audrey II all over the world.

CHRISTOPHER GUEST
as First Customer

A NATIVE NEW YORKER, GUEST studied clarinet at the High School of Music and Art, then moved into comedy as a satirist for the magazine *National Lampoon* and its companion radio show. Moving on to television, he won an Emmy as writer of Lily Tomlin's first comedy special in which he also co-starred. Turning to acting, he appeared in the popular TV series *Laverne and Shirley* and

All in the Family and took dramatic parts in *Blind Ambition*, based on John Dean's autobiography, where he appeared as Jeb Magruder. His feature films include *The Long Riders* (1980), *Girlfriends* (1978) and *Heartbeeps* (1981) as well as Rob Reiner's satiric rockumentary *This is Spinal Tap* (1984).

BILL MURRAY
as Arthur Denton

MURRAY MAKES A BRIEF BUT memorable appearance as a masochistic dental patient, a role made famous in the original *Little Shop* by Jack Nicholson. The role, incidentally, was excised from the off-Broadway show, but reinserted in the film version. The character's name, however, was changed from Wilbur Force to Arthur Denton, reminiscent of the nebbish high school student, Walter Denton, portrayed by Richard Crenna in the '50s TV sitcom *Our Miss Brooks*. The Illinois-born Murray gave up premed studies to join Chicago's *Second*

City improvisational troupe. After touring for a few years with the group's road company, he moved on to New York and became part of *The National Lampoon Show* off-Broadway. His co-stars included John Belushi, Gilda Radner and Harold Ramis. Murray was signed for ABC's short-lived *Saturday Night Live with Howard Cosell*, which hit the airwaves shortly before NBC's more familiar *Saturday Night Live*. After the former show failed, *SNL* producer Lorne Michaels brought Murray on board. He made his feature film debut as a spaced-out camp counselor in the smash hit *Meatballs* (1979) then went on to appear as the stoned-out journalist Hunter Thompson in *Where the Buffalo Roam* (1980). His other films include: *Caddyshack* (1980), *Stripes* (1981), *Tootsie* (1982), *Ghostbusters* (1984), and *The Razor's Edge* (1984), an ambitious adaptation of the Somerset Maugham novel in which he tackled his first dramatic role. He also co-scripted the film, which proved to be a box-office failure.

JOHN CANDY
as Wink Wilkenson

LIKE RICK MORANIS, THE TORONTO-born Candy gained fame on the syndicated *SCTV* show, where he won two Emmys for comedy writing. He made his film debut in *Class of '44*, the 1973 sequel to the popular *Summer of '42* (1972). The rotund Candy is more well known, however, for his appearances in the hit comedies *The Blues Brothers* (1980), *Stripes* (1981), *National Lampoon's Vacation* (1983), *Splash* (1984), *Brewster's Millions* (1985) and *Volunteers* (1985). The part of radio announcer Wink Wilkenson in *Little Shop*, a character that does not appear in the off-Broadway show, was created for him.

The Making of
Little Shop of
Horrors

THE LIKELY EXPLANATION FOR Steven Spielberg's bow-out of the *Little Shop* movie (apart from his multifarious other commitments) was his inability to acquire the film rights to the off-Broadway show for his own company, Amblin' Entertainment. David Geffen, co-backer of the musical, had already acquired the rights for his own firm, The Geffen Film Company, which had been quite active in film production since the early eighties. Geffen's company had produced Robert Towne's *Personal Best* (1982), the cult youth comedy *Risky Business* (1983), which catapulted Tom Cruise to fame, Albert Brooks' yuppy version of *Easy Rider, Lost in America* (1985), and Martin Scorsese's urban black comedy, *After Hours* (1985).

Geffen's career reads like a showbiz cliche.

John Candy makes a cameo appearance as dee-jay Weird Wink Wilkenson, who introduces Seymour and Audrey II to the people in radioland.

He started out in 1964 as a clerk in the mail room of the William Morris Agency, one of the largest talent agencies in the world. Four years later, he formed his own talent agency, Geffen-Roberts Management, with Elliott Roberts, another William Morris alumnus, representing music industry clients such as Joni Mitchell, Crosby, Stills, Nash and Young, as well as Jackson Browne. In 1971, he formed his own record label, Asylum Records, later merging it with Elektra to form Elektra/Asylum. The Eagles, Linda Ronstadt, Jackson Browne, Queen, Carly Simon, Bob Dylan and many others performed for the new label. Then, four years after that, he left the music industry to join Warner Brothers' film division as Vice President, overseeing the production of the George Burns' comedy, *Oh, God!* (1977), Robert Benton's *The Late Show* (1977) with Art Carney and Lily Tomlon, and Richard Pryor's *Greased Lightning* (1977). He also taught a course on the music business at UCLA and Yale University. In 1980, he returned to the music business, creating another label, Geffen Records, for which he signed John Lennon and Yoko Ono, Donna Summer, Elton John, and Peter Gabriel. He also began backing Broadway shows. His first, the late Michael Bennett's *Dreamgirls*, was a smash hit—as was his next show, the award-winning *Cats* by Andrew Lloyd-Webber. Then came *Little Shop of Horrors*.

Having assumed control of the *Little Shop* movie himself and secured a distribution deal with Warner Bros., Geffen approached Frank Oz to direct. It was unquestionably an ideal choice.

Oz began his entertainment career in partnership with Jim Henson. Together, they had created the Muppets. Oz himself provided the vocal characterizations for Miss Piggy, Fozzie Bear, Animal, Cookie Monster, and Bert and Grover on *Sesame Street*, Henson's syndicated *The Muppet Show* and *The Muppet Movie* (1979). Oz also played bit parts —in *The Blues Brothers*, *Trading Places* and John Landis' special effects laden *An American Werewolf in London* (1981). Apart from the Muppet characters with whom he is so closely identified, Oz is, perhaps, best known for his vocal characterization of Yoda, the aging and wrinkled tutor of the Jedi Knights in *The Empire Strikes Back* (1980) and *Return of the Jedi* (1983), the second and third installments in George Lucas' blockbuster *Star Wars* trilogy. Subsequently, Oz served as co-producer (as well as supplying many of the voices) on the second Muppet movie, *The Great Muppet Caper* (1981) which Jim Henson directed himself. The pair put aside the Muppet characters temporarily in 1983 to make a different kind of puppet fantasy, the epic *The Dark Crystal*, which Oz co-directed. For the next

big screen Muppet adventure, *The Muppets Take Manhattan* (1984), Oz moved completely into the director's chair. His expertise in combining sometimes spectacular song and dance routines with ingenious special effects—puppetry [or Muppetry] and animatronics—in this film and others would serve him well on the *Little Shop* movie.

Ironically though, Oz was initially reluctant to take the project on. "I looked at the script and said 'No,'" he told *The Los Angeles Times*' Jack Mathews. "I didn't think I could get my hands around it. There were too many elements. It was a period piece, there were fourteen songs and a puppet that was going to weigh a ton." In addition, big budget movie musicals —most recently John Huston's *Annie* (1980)—had not fared well at the box-office. But with some persuasion from Geffen, Oz gradually warmed to the project, eventually finding it— so to speak—"right up his alley."

In transferring the musical to the screen, Oz decided early on to eschew the kind of campy approach that had made *The Rocky Horror Picture Show* such a cult hit. "Camp is cold," he said. "[It] has no warmth, keeps you at a distance. The essence of camp is that people make fun of the material and imply they are superior to what they are doing. In this film, I want [the audience] to believe in the characters, to laugh with the people, and not at them. What I am trying to achieve is a 'heightened reality.'" He was also determined not to alter the concept of the off-Broadway show in any way—a goal which, as we shall see, eventually proved unattainable.

Another decision that was made early on was to shoot the film in England. There were a number of reasons for this, not the least of them being economic. The budget for the film was set at $17 million* and at the time (November-December '85), exchange rates between the British pound and the American dollar were quite favorable. Stanley Kubrick, who shot his $17 million Vietnam epic *Full Metal Jacket* (1987) entirely in London, is very upfront about this. "Hollywood's probably the best technically," he says. "But it's more expensive to make movies there. London's the second best, but you get more on the screen for the same money."

Little Shop line producer Bill Gilmore insists that money wasn't the only concern, however. "The key to this movie is the plant," he told the *New York Times*. "There is a whole new skill grown up in Britain since

Star Wars called animatronics. Basically, it is the art of making creatures that have a life of their own."

Yet another reason for the move to England was space. To achieve Oz's 'heightened reality,' production designer Roy Walker* was challenged with creating an ultra-realistic skid row set, complete with littered alleyways, ramshackle tenements buildings and *West Side Story* rooftops—even an elevated train seen at a distance. To do this, he needed a very large sound stage—the largest in the world, in fact. That sound stage, built to accommodate Ken Adams' breathtaking sets for the James Bond films—and dubbed the "007

As Seymour (Rick Moranis) waits to go on the air with Wink Wilkenson, the vampiric Audrey II attempts to put the bite on an unwary secretary.

---

*Estimates of the film's final cost have gone as high as $40 million, but Warner Bros., David Geffen and Frank Oz emphatically deny this. The elaborate animatronic and other effects did push the film over budget, but more to the tune of $26 million, they say. For a film to be characterized as a hit, the standard rule of thumb is that it must earn back *triple* its original budget in order to accommodate print and advertising costs. As of May 6, 1987—roughly six months after the film's release—*Variety* reported that *Little Shop* had taken in only $12 million in U.S. and Canadian rentals. Though doing well overseas, the film, despite all the critical accolades, will probably take quite some time to get into the black.

*Walker won an Oscar for his art direction on Stanley Kubrick's *Barry Lyndon* (1975) and was nominated for his work on Barbra Streisand's *Yentl* (1983). Roland Joffe's Oscar-winning *The Killing Fields* (1984) is listed among his other credits.

Behind the scenes on Little Shop of Horrors. From left to right: Ellen Greene, Frank Oz, Rick Moranis.

Frank Oz lines up a shot on the set of the Little Shop of Horrors.

Stage"—is located at Pinewood Studios in Buckinghamshire, outside London. George Lucas shot interiors for is *Star Wars* trilogy there, as well as for *Raiders of the Lost Ark* (1981) and its "prequel," *Indiana Jones and the Temple of Doom* (1984). For *Little Shop*, the "007 Stage" was turned into skid row.

Walker sent set decorator Tessa Davies to New York on a scavenger hunt to find gas meters, soap boxes, doorknobs, street signs and literally hundreds of other vintage 1960 East Side New York props. Davies says the most difficult items she had to find were garbage cans from that era. "They had to be genuine and they had to be old," she says. "I went around the streets in a truck loaded with new garbage cans, offering to trade them for used ones. People thought I was crazy."

At the same time, costume designer Marit Allen began rummaging through thrift shops to come up with sixties-style clothes. "What helped," she says, "was that all the principals had a definite idea of how they should dress—particularly Ellen Greene, who wanted clothes that looked like they might have been cast off by Kim Novak or Rita Hayworth. We agreed that there would be a point in the story where her image would change. When she falls in love with Seymour, she goes from red, black and leopard skins to softer shades. Likewise, Rick Moranis' wardrobe was designed to help Seymour bridge the credibility gap, somewhere between a nerdy loser and a shy, appealing guy."

Apart from the elaborate set

From left to right: producer David Geffen, Rick Moranis, director Frank Oz and Ellen Greene.

design, the main challenge faced by the film's creators was the plant itself —Audrey II. Martin P. Robinson's deceptively simple sleight-of-hand puppet tricks, which had worked so well off-Broadway, would not pass muster with film audiences used to the eye-popping (and mind boggling) creature effects perfected in such films as *Aliens* (1986) and others. And so the job of creating an Audrey II that would literally blow the audience away was handed to acknowledged animatronics wizard Lyle Conway, an expatriate American living in England.

Conway had worked previously with Frank Oz, as well as Jim Henson, on *The Dark Crystal* and television's *The Muppet Show*. His other film credits include Disney's *Return to Oz* (1985). In search of inspiration, Con-way visited London's famous Kew Gardens. "I felt that at each stage of her development, Audrey II [had to have] a distinct look," he says. "The baby plant looked like a rosebud [with lips modeled after Ellen Greene's]." As the plant grows and becomes more monstrous, it also becomes more top heavy. To solve this problem, Conway turned to England's Atomic Energy Authority for technical advice on creating a core that would support and control the creature. "The scientists there saw it as a game," he says. "A pleasant break from their top security work. They were immensely helpful. Size is the downfall of most mechanical marvels. Small creatures are relatively easy. Big ones suffer from gravity. The challenge was to take something twelve and a half feet tall, weighing slightly more than one ton and make it rap and boogie with a life of its own." To get these effects right, particularly the lip synching, took as many as fifty puppeteers working together all at one time. By the time Conway's work was finished, he'd gone through 15,000 handmade leaves, 2000 feet of vine, hundreds of gallons of KY Jelly, 4½ tons of latex and 11½ miles of cable. "Just slightly more than was used to build the Brooklyn Bridge," he says.

Each special effects sequence involving Audrey II was storyboarded ahead of time by former Marvel Comics artist Mike Ploog, who had performed similar chores on Richard Lester's *Superman II* (1980) and the Steven Spielberg production of *Young Sherlock Holmes* (1985). Nevertheless, Oz says, the plant sequences took up a lot of shooting time. "It was a very painstaking process. The last number ["Mean Green Mother From Outer Space"] alone took five weeks to shoot. But you can't underestimate audiences these days. They expect effects to look *real*. If one little thing is off, you can lose the whole scene." Literally an army of technicians— over 100—were involved in creating the film's host of puppet, animation and animatronic effects. 63 people alone are listed in the film's credits as "principal" and "additional" plant performers. Levi Stubbs, an original member of the Four Tops, further fleshed out the character of Audrey II by giving the plant its voice and singing its numbers.

Howard Ashman's screenplay follows his off-Broadway show fairly closely so there is no need to recount the basic storyline, which, until the film's conclusion, is virtually identical. Befitting the new medium, Oz "opens up" the show, but not to excess. "I didn't want to balloon it into a musical *War and Peace* or a '40s extravaganza," he says. "There are no dizzying overhead crane shots [except in the beginning for the number "Downtown"]. No irrelevant dance numbers. Nothing to overwhelm what is basically the simple story of a boy, a girl and a man-eating plant." Oz's staging, particularly some of the early musical numbers, and the use of the street urchins as a travelling Greek Chorus is patterned quite closely after Ashman's original staging.

The score and vocalizations are also quite similar. In his solos, Rick Moranis sounds remarkably like Lee Wilkof, the originator of the role off-Broadway, just as Wilkof had sounded remarkably like Jonathan Haze, the originator of the role in Corman's film. Steve Martin brings a lot more Elvis—as well as Steve Martin-style gusto—to the role of the sadistic dentist, Orin Scrivello. He slugs his nurse with his fist and a door, twists the head off the doll of a child patient, and, in an homage to the Corman film, runs amusingly headlong into a masochistic patient, Arthur Denton, whom Scrivello finally throws out of his office in frustration because the guy is such a "sicko." For many, this scene is one of the comic high points of the new *Little Shop of Horrors*. There's no denying it's funny. But in the authors' humble view, Jack

Nicholson's pain-loving Wilbur Force seemed a lot crazier than Bill Murray's relatively low-key Arthur Denton and so the scene in the original film remains, for us anyway, a lot funnier.

Where the film departs mostly— and suffers a bit because of it—is in the elimination of three key songs. A fourth song, "Don't Feed the Plants," was also eliminated and replaced by an original, "Mean Green Mother From Outer Space." But more about that later.

The three key songs that are deleted are: "Mushnik and Son"; "Now (It's Just the Gas)," the duet performed by Seymour and Scrivello when Seymour attempts to shoot him with a gun; and "The Meek Shall Inherit." The latter song is synthesized into a short dialogue sequence in which James Belushi makes a cameo appearance as Patrick Martin, the botanical entrepreneur who tries to sell Seymour on the idea of making cuttings of Audrey II and marketing them all over the world.

The elimination of "Mushnik and Son" is the most serious deletion. It is one of the show's funniest numbers, but more importantly, this duet sung by Seymour and Mushnik, the flower shop owner, serves to keep Mushnik in focus as an important central character. Toned down in the off-Broadway show, Mushnik, in the film, fairly disappears. He is a minor presence—whereas in Corman's original, particularly as played by Mel Welles, Mushnik emerged not only as a major character, but arguably the funniest and most memorable character in the film. It's *his* lines that

are most often quoted by *Little Shop* buffs. Corman is right when he says that while the new Mushnik gets some laughs, the old Mushnik (Welles) got, and still gets, a lot more. In many ways, Vincent Gardenia's Mushnik might as well have been cut from the film, for the character, especially without that one song, is given fairly little to do—except get eaten by Audrey II. When the film is over, one almost forgets the character existed. This is not true of Moranis's endearingly waif-like Seymour, Ellen Greene's put-upon Audrey and Steve Martin's flamboyant Scrivello. In fact, most reviewers felt it was Martin, not even the plant, who truly stole the show.

As we know, the off-Broadway show ended, as did the Corman original, with the guilt-ridden Seymour committing suicide by climbing inside the now gigantic plant and trying to carve it up. [In the show, remember, Audrey herself dies as a result of being mauled by the plant, adding to Seymour's guilt and despair.] Following this, the plant's petals open to reveal the faces of its victims, singing a warning shout to the audience not to feed the plants.

Ashman's screenplay concluded the same way—but with a more spectacular special effects scene of Audrey II chomping down on everyone, its tendrils bursting through the walls of the shop like something out of John Carpenter's *The Thing* (1982). Its petals open, but rather than faces, they reveal myriad Audrey IIs, screeching and sticking out their tongues like Linda Blair in *The Exor-*

Scrivello (Steve Martin) examines the mouth of a patient with fiendish delight.

"They hated us when the main characters died," Oz says. "In the play, they're eaten by the puppet, but

cist (1973). Once the characters have all succumbed to Audrey II's shark-like teeth, the plant bursts from the flower shop and is last seen strolling across the Brooklyn Bridge on its way to devour the world. These scenes were shot at great expense, but were later cut from the film and replaced when, during a sneak preview, audiences, heretofore delighted with film, grew visibly angry and upset

you know they're coming out for a curtain call. But the power of movies is different. They really believed in those characters and were very angry. I wanted to stay true to the play, but after that screening, I felt that the play's last act was not translatable. It had to have a happy ending. It was not a matter of Warner Bros. and Geffen saying you have to do it and the director pounding his fist on the table. They did say I had to do it, but I wanted to."

like cottage in the suburbs far away from skid row. But then the camera peers down among the foliage surrounding the fence, and there, lurking

Oz, Moranis, Greene and crew went back to Pinewood and re-shot a new ending where Seymour electrocutes the carnivorous mammoth, destroying the shop in the process, and emerges from the ashes like a diminutive superhero. Recalling Audrey's fantasy number "Somewhere That's Green," the pair is last seen entering the longed-for, cartoon-

among the flora, is another Audrey II the size of a small bulb. And it breaks into its familiar grin. In effect, Oz managed to have it both ways—a happy ending with a little sting in the tail. He also managed to leave the door open for a sequel.

Whether there *will* be a sequel or not [there have been rumors] depends in large part on the film's box-office tally once it has finished playing off in other markets. As already mentioned, it did not become the megahit in the U.S. and Canada that Warner Bros. had hoped—despite good word-of-mouth and good reviews. In fact, after its debut in December '86, the film all but dropped out of sight—at least until the summer drive-in season. It was almost as if Warner Bros. and/or exhibitors had lost faith in it, an idea suggested shortly after the film's release by an unnamed writer in California's *Orange Coast* Magazine, who noted:

> Warner Bros. has drastically altered its expectations of *Little Shop of Horrors*, a $30 million comic musical extravaganza adapted from the hit Broadway [sic] play. At one time, the studio considered this to be their big prestigious, winter project, filled with celebrity cameo appearances, a dozen or so bouncy songs and a fun, silly story. The perfect ingredients for a $100 million success. Or so they thought. Well, maybe not. Warner Bros. has suddenly realized that while this film does make for enjoyable light entertainment, it's just not the sort of thing that people line up around the block for. What that means to Warners is that they better start covering their losses.

* * *

At the 1986 Academy Awards ceremony held in March of 1987, *Little Shop*'s awareness factor got a tem-porary boost when "Mean Green Mother From Outer Space," the new song Ashman and Menken had written expressly for the movie, was nominated in the Best Original Song category. Levi Stubbs, numerous dancers and a mock-up of Audrey II were all on hand to perform the number on the stage of the Dorothy Chandler Pavilion for the live telecast. The song lost, however, to one of two songs nominated from Paramount's summer blockbuster, *Top Gun* (1986).

Ironically, the film's fortunes genuinely shot skyward when it was released some months later on video, where it became a top seller and rental for many weeks. Perhaps, when all is said and done, the truth is that audiences respond best to *Little Shop* as a movie on the small screen—where its reputation was first made.

Roger Corman, ever the entrepreneur, sees still a lot more life in the old plant yet, however, as witness the following item culled from the January 20, 1986 edition of *Variety* under the

Seymour (Rick Moranis) sings a duet with Audrey II.

heading "Corman Lands WB Licensing Deal on 'Shop'":

> Roger Corman has struck a licensing deal on his 1960 pic, *The Little Shop of Horrors*, with Warner Bros. The pact was jointly announced as covering 'certain media,' but Corman's Concorde Pictures said Warners will handle the original *Little Shop* through almost all distribution conduits on Corman's behalf. However, the deal allows Corman to put his film back into the marketplace for six months after Warner's release of the Geffen Film Co. pic. Corman, who has seen his $30,000 film bring in $6-$7,000,000 in estimated receipts and bookings, and 'has never stopped booking,' stressed, 'We'll be there very strongly' following the six-month term."

So look out Audrey II! You may be getting some competition in the not too distant future from your ancestor, Audrey Jr., as the phenomenon that is *The Little Shop of Horrors* continues to grow...and grow!

The street urchins (Tichina Arnold, Tisha Campbell and Michelle Weeks) warn Mushnik (Vincent Gardenia) of what's coming.

« *Little Shop* »
on *Record,*
Video, and in Print

Record

The Little Shop of Horrors: The complete score by Fred Katz from the 1960 Roger Corman film. Available from: Maniac Music (Starlog Press), 475 Park Avenue South, 8th Floor, New York, NY 10016. A must! (Listeners really get four for the price of one, as the Katz score was also used in Corman's *Creature from the Haunted Sea*, *A Bucket of Blood*, and *The Wasp Woman*.)

Little Shop of Horrors: Original off-Broadway Cast Album). Album produced by Phil Ramone. Available from: Geffen Records, 9126 Sunset Blvd., Los Angeles, CA 90096. (Manufactured exclusively by Warner Bros. Records, Inc., a Warner Communications Company.) In addition to all the songs, the album also includes portions of dialogue from the off-Broadway musical. A must for those who didn't see the original show and want to compare it with the movie version. Also available on audio cassette.

The cover of the comic book tie-in to the big screen version of Howard Ashman's off-Broadway success, Little Shop of Horrors.

A video magazine announces the release of Frank Oz's spectacular big screen version of the musical Little Shop of Horrors. *Now everyone can enjoy this zany film in the comfort of his own home.*

Steve Martin as sadistic dentist Orin Scrivello, the "Leader of the Plaque."

Little Shop of Horrors: (The Original Motion Picture Soundtrack). Available from: Geffen Records, 9126 Sunset Blvd., Los Angeles, CA 90096. (Manufactured by Warner Bros. Records, a Warner Communications Company.) Also available on cassette and compact disc. Includes the Oscar-nominated song "Mean Green Mother from Outer Space" written especially for the film by Howard Ashman. Album features entire cast: Rick Moranis, Ellen Greene, Vincent Gardenia, Steve Martin, et. al.

Video

The Little Shop of Horrors: Colorized version of the 1960 Roger Corman film. Available from: Vestron Video, 60 Long Ridge Road, P.O. Box 4000, Stamford, CT 06907. VHS and Beta. The black and white version is also available in both formats (at a much cheaper price) from a host of public domain sources. 70 minutes.

Little Shop of Horrors: The 1986 movie version of the off-Broadway play. A Geffen Co. release through Warner Bros. of a Geffen Co. Production. Available from: Warner Home Video, 4000 Warner Blvd., Burbank, CA 91522. VHS and Beta. Hi-Fi Stereo. 88 minutes.

Print

Little Shop of Horrors: Book and lyrics by Howard Ashman. Music by Alan Menken. The complete libretto of the off-Broadway musical. Available from: The Samuel French Theater Bookshop, 45 West 25th Street, New York, NY 10010. Volume also includes a good deal of background information on the creation of Martin P. Robinson's puppetry effects.

Little Shop of Horrors: The official comic book adaptation (tie-in) of the 1986 Warner Bros. movie. Script adaptation by Michael Fleisher. Art by Gene Colan & Dave Hunt. Coloring by Anthony Tollin. Lettering by John Costanza. Editor: Julius Schwartz. Available from: DC Comics.

Little Shop of Horrors: By Robert and Louise Egan, based on the screenplay by Howard Ashman. "Photonovel" tie-in to the hit 1986 movie with text and 156 b&w photos from the film. 79 pages. Available from: Perigee Books (The Putnam Publishing Group), 200 Madison Avenue, New York, NY 10016.

Bibliography

Books

Ashman, Howard and Menken, Alan. *Little Shop of Horrors*. New York: Samuel French, Inc., 1985

McCarthy, Todd and Flynn, Charles. *Kings of the Bs*. New York: E.P. Dutton, Inc., 1975

McGee, Mark Thomas. *Fast and Furious: The Story of American International Pictures*. North Carolina: McFarland & Company, Inc., 1984

Naha, Ed. *The Films of Roger Corman*. New York: Arco Publishing, Inc., 1982

Peary, Danny. *Cult Movies*. New York: Delta, 1981

Warren, Bill. *Keep Watching the Skies!* (Vol. II). North Carolina: McFarland & Company, Inc., 1986

Miscellaneous Reviews

Commonweal: Vol. 114, 1/30/87, pp. 55

Glamour: Vol. 85, 2/87, pp. 175

High Fidelity: Vol. 33, 7/83, pp. 95

Horizon: Vol. 27, 3/84, pp. 47

Los Angeles: Vol. 28, 6/83, pp. 56

MaClean's: Vol. 100, 1/5/87, pp. 18

New Republic: Vol. 196, 1/26/87, pp. 26

New Statesman: Vol. 106, 10/21/83, pp. 30

Newsweek: Vol. 109, 1/5/87, pp. 56

New York: Vol. 20, 1/12/87, pp. 51

New Yorker: Vol. 26, 1/12/87, pp. 92

Penthouse: Vol. 14, 6/83, pp. 50

People Weekly: Vol. 27, 1/12/87, pp. 10

Playboy: Vol. 34, 3/87, pp. 19

Stereo Review: Vol. 48, 4/83, pp. 91

Time: Vol. 128, 12/29/86, pp. 71

Variety: Vol. 325, 12/10/86, pp. 14

Wall St. Journal: 12/23/86, pp. 18

Periodicals

Anonymous: "Laughing Gas," *Los Angeles Herald Examiner*, 2/3/87

Anonymous: *Little Shop of Horrors*," *Los Angeles*, Vol. 28, 4/83, pp. 58

Anonymous: "Little Shop returning to the screen," *NY Times*, 8/23/85, pp. 21

Anonymous: "Original 'Horrors' to make vid debut," *Hollywood Reporter*, 12/18/86

Anonymous: "Shop Season," *Hollywood Reporter*, 12/18/86

Anonymous: "WB buys Little Shop," *Variety*, Vol. 325, 8/10/85

Billington, Michael: "New life for Little Shop," *NY Times*, 12/8/85, pp. 14

Bonansinga, Jay: "The Little Shop of Horrors," *Filmfax*, Vol. 1, No. 5, pp. 26-28

Dunn, Donald H.: "The best shows — and bargains—may be off-Broadway," *Business Week*, 1/24/83, pp. 79

Everitt, David: "Little Shop of Horrors," *Fangoria*, Vol. 3, No. 3, pp. 45-49

Klein, Richard: "Corman lands WB licensing deal on 'Shop'," *Variety*, Vol. 325, 1/20/86, pp. 1, 28

Mathews, Jack: "Director Frank Oz goes for the comedy of horrors," *Los Angeles Times*, 12/19/86, pp. 1, 10

McGee, Mark Thomas: *Charles Griffith and the Little Shop of Corman*," *Fangoria*, Vol. 2, No. 11, pp. 16-17, 62

Nutman, Philip: "Little Shop of Lyle conway," *Fangoria*, Vol. 5, No. 62, pp. 42-46

Pirani, Adam: "Remaking Little Shop of Horrors," *Fangoria*, Vol. 4, No. 60, pp. 34-38

Powers, John: *Bleak Chic*," *American Film*, Vol. 12, No. 5, pp. 46-51

Sharbutt, Jay: "Will this plant be a star in New York?," *Los Angeles Herald Examiner*, 7/11/83, pp. 3, 6

Weaver, Tom and Brunas, John: "The original Mushnick," *Fangoria*, Vol. 4, No. 58, pp. 14-17, 62

Williams, Sharon: "The Jonathan Haze Story," *Filmfax*, Vol. 1, No. 5, pp. 30-38, 54-57

Willman, Chris: "A slimy problem," *Los Angeles Times*, 3/1/87

Wilson, John M.: "Packing a pistil," *Los Angeles Times*, 10/5/86

Authors

JOHN McCARTY is the author of seven books on the film and broadcast media. Including, most recently, *Splatter Movies: Breaking the Last Taboo of the Screen* (St. Martin's Press, 1984); *Alfred Hitchcock Presents* (St. Martin's Press, 1985); *Psychos: 80 Years of Mad Movies, Maniacs and Murderous Deeds* (St. Martin's Press, 1986); and *The Films of John Huston* (Citadel Press, 1987). He lives in upstate New York.

MARK THOMAS McGEE, a frequent contributor to *Monsterland* and *Fangoria* magazines, is the author of three books on film. They include: *The J.D. Films – A History of Juvenile Delinquency in Motion Pictures* (McFarland, 1984); *Fast and Furious – The Story of American International Pictures* (McFarland, 1984); and the upcoming *Roger Corman – Best of the Cheap Acts* (McFarland, 1988). He lives in California.